TROLLS

TROLLS
AN UNNATURAL HISTORY

JOHN LINDOW

REAKTION BOOKS

For my family, and to the memory of Alan Dundes

Published by Reaktion Books Ltd
33 Great Sutton Street
London EC1V ODX, UK

www.reaktionbooks.co.uk

First published 2014

Printed and bound in Great Britain
by TJ International, Padstow, Cornwall

A catalogue record for this book is available from the British Library

ISBN 978 1 78023 289 8

Contents

Erik Werenskiold, a plucky hero and a three-headed troll,
illustration from 'Soria Moria Castle'.

Introduction

Back in the 1970s, an acquaintance learned that I was interested in folklore and things Scandinavian. She had, she said, a story that I might like to hear. On a rainy September evening when she was an exchange student in Oslo, she went to have dinner with some Norwegian friends and thoroughly enjoyed herself. Waiting for the last tram of the night to take her home, she 'experienced' (her word) a troll. She was standing on the platform looking down the tracks when the troll appeared above the treetops, a few hundred metres away. He (so she referred to it) stood and bowed his head and waved to her slowly with his left hand. At just that moment, the wind died down completely. She was, she said, simultaneously fascinated and frightened. The troll seemed to have some kind of magnetic power, and she could not take her eyes off him. She could not tell what, if anything, he was wearing, given the darkness, but she knew that he had to be tall, and thought that he had long shaggy hair and very little neck. For perhaps as long as three minutes, she stared at the troll, but when the light of the approaching tram appeared, he vanished, and the wind started blowing again. When she got home, she recounted the event in her diary, writing in Norwegian the words: 'experienced a troll while I was waiting for the tram'.

The next day she discussed the experience with some friends, although when I spoke to her she wasn't sure what exactly they had said. She did tell me that if it wasn't a troll, it might have been a tree. The whole experience was, however, uncanny.

Part of my satisfaction in learning about this experience was that it follows nearly perfectly the paradigm worked out by (primarily

Nordic) folklorists, and best articulated by the Finnish folklorist and historian of religion Lauri Honko, for encounters with the empirical supernatural: that is, it explains how perfectly rational people could see things that most of us don't usually think could be there. The model uses rather simple theories of cognition: a person who is under some kind of stress or in a state of conflict or a conducive psycho-physical condition (induced, for example, by fatigue or consumption of alcohol), and operating within a certain frame of reference, is confronted with an incomplete 'releasing' stimulus, usually involving only one sense. Using traditional means of cognition, the person complements the stimulus – creates, as it were, complementing stimuli – and experiences a vision. Frequently the circumstances do not aid sensory input; for example, it may be dark. Interpretation follows, frequently involving social control or the opinions of others. Thus if we hear noises in a graveyard we may imagine ghosts, but in a dangerous part of town such sounds could indicate a person of dubious character, such as a mugger. If we recount to our friends that we heard/saw a ghost in the dark of night in some sketchy urban neighbourhood, they might insist that it was more likely to have been a mugger. In neither case, for us, would a troll be likely.

If, however, we look at my friend's experience in this light, we can see how and why she may have 'experienced' her troll. Rain and wind compounded the darkness of night, and she had had some beer at dinner. The 'releasing' stimulus was primarily visual, although she also commented on the sudden dying down of the wind; this we should probably understand as her realization that she was in the presence of something uncanny, even numinous (she was at once fascinated and frightened). The light on the front of the approaching tram helped her rearrange the visual stimuli, and the vision dis-appeared.

As regards possible stress we can only speculate, but it seems likely that this young woman's national identity was an issue for her. She was an American in the process of acquiring a Norwegian identity, as is linguistically manifest in her use of both languages in her diary. The switch to Norwegian at precisely the moment when she recorded her experience with the troll connects it to the Norwegian side of her identity. No American would expect to see *that* kind of troll, but my friend seemed to think that Norwegians might, and her Norwegian friends apparently said nothing to dissuade her the following day. We may think of my friend as being sufficiently modern to question her own experience (perhaps it was a tree?), but in other times and places people certainly have had similar doubts. Part of the model I have just sketched is that alternative views remain possible.

This model is important. It helps us to understand that in many cultures supernatural beings can indeed be part of people's empirical experience. Trolls were not just found in books: they were also in the landscape, to be glimpsed from time to time.

Trolls are everywhere today. Everyone knows what a troll is, even if our personal notions of trolls might differ. It is fair to say that the troll has been one of the most powerful and enduring images of otherness in large parts of the world, with a resonance that is inescapable.

For centuries, however, trolls were found only in the landscape of Scandinavia. They were 'nature beings'; that is, beings who were encountered in nature. Their home environment was a pre-industrial society in which people lived by farming and fishing, often on a small scale. Scandinavia is, of course, a big place; it is often said that it is further from Oslo to the north cape of Norway than to Rome. It is also a lot further from the Swedish-speaking parts of Finland to Iceland than it is from, say, southern Jutland in Denmark to Sicily. There are now five Nordic nation states and three autonomous regions with eight national languages. There are forests and tundra, fertile flat lands and towering mountains, rivers, lakes and oceans. Yet despite all this size and consequent variation, there have always been essential similarities of culture, not least in the areas of folklore and 'folk belief' (more on the inverted commas below), where trolls lived and functioned. These similarities existed in spite of regional variations of social organization (such as village systems in the south and separated farmsteads in the north).

The early chapters of this book will focus on poems and stories, especially on the kind of stories that folklorists call *legends*. Essentially, these are more or less believable stories, set in the here and now. The folklorist Jan Brunvand collected stories of this kind from contemporary American culture in such books as *The Vanishing*

Hitchhiker (1981), *The Choking Doberman* (1984) and *The Mexican Pet* (1986), titles that give some indication of the kinds of story to which I am referring. You or I may not believe that someone could mistake a large rat for a little dog from Mexico, which is exactly what happens in *The Mexican Pet*, but lots of people have done, and I have heard the story told as true. Brunvand called the stories he collected 'urban legends', thus separating them from the rural legends in which trolls feature, but in the end they are all just legends. Our legends are contemporary to us; troll legends were contemporary to the people who told and listened to them.

When talking about legends I will also rely on a notion of 'folk belief'. As a scholarly term, 'folk belief' originated in the early twentieth century, but it was presaged by a distinction that goes back to the Brothers Grimm. They once wrote that the *Märchen* (folk tale or fairy tale; we lack an accurate term in English) was 'more poetic' and the legend was 'more historical'. By 'more historical' they presumably meant 'more realistic' or 'more believable'. The latter conception helps us think of legends as one of the forms in which 'folk belief' manifests itself. We may define 'folk belief' as a shared system of views and conceptions about the world in which people live. It is shorthand for what we, as observers, can extrapolate from the cultural artefacts we seek to analyse. We now understand that we cannot really know what anyone believed, or even that individual belief was or is always consistent. Here I like to think about an Icelander called Helgi the Lean, who converted to Christianity 1,000 years ago. Even after his conversion he continued to call upon the god Thor (usually construed as Christ's enemy, but associated with wind and violent weather) when he was at sea. I once found myself wondering whether I should give Thor a chance when I was high up on a mountain during a thunderstorm.

Nor can we reconstruct common beliefs in a 'folk', since that concept too is highly elastic. Early folklorists construed the 'folk' as identical to 'the nation', but as the field matured it became clear that most of us are members of many 'folks': clubs, occupational groups, hobby groups, families, regional groups and so forth, and that we can go back and forth between groups. What we can talk about is 'the believable' in a given discourse community. What is believable is contested, and the more or less believable narratives about trolls and similar phenomena should be taken not as the 'beliefs' of a 'folk' but rather as small pieces of a much larger discussion about the nature of the environment in which people lived. Legends are not told in formal storytelling events ('Once upon a time'). Rather, they crop up when individuals are conversing. Thus they relate to conversational topics, are told within the give and take of conversation, and may be intended to persuade, amuse or amaze. The legends we now have about trolls, however, were collected by folklorists in rural areas in Scandinavia, mostly in the nineteenth and twentieth centuries. Because they are thus cut off from the original conversational contexts, we must content ourselves with looking at what they say, rather than how or why they say it.

When we investigate the meaning of a word, we frequently and naturally ask ourselves what it originally meant. Trolls, however, have kept their secret, and we still do not know the origin of the word *troll*. Guesses include derivation from such verbs as 'tread', 'to rush away angrily', 'roll' (as with ball lightning) and 'enchant', as well as from a noun meaning 'stout person'. While we can perhaps conjure up images of trolls to which any of the above might be applied, I incline towards an origin related to magic, especially shifting and changing things, on the basis of material that will become apparent in the chapters that follow. If nothing else, this explanation agrees with the lexical situation: like trolls themselves, the word seems to have been capable of shape- and even gender-shifting. Old Norse (the language of Norway and Iceland during the later Middle Ages) shows two forms, *troll* and *trǫll* (both neuter in grammatical gender). Rhymes in the older poetry guarantee both forms, although there is only one instance of the second. On the other hand, that form became the modern Icelandic word (*tröll* in the modern orthography), and Faroese has a parallel form *trøll*. Norwegian has *troll* and Danish has *trold* (common gender, that is, not neuter, like all the other forms cited). Swedish has *troll* (neuter) from older *trull* (also neuter). It is not possible to derive all these forms from a single underlying source, although historical phonology can make sense of many of them. The gender may be less tricky: the Danish common gender presumably has to do with a sense that neuter gender is inappropriate for beings with human form.

In Old Norse, the word *troll/trǫll* denoted all sorts of things – giants, troublesome people, even troublesome animals – as we shall see in the next chapter. This semantic breadth adds to the problem of determining the etymology or even the primary meaning of troll, but it is emblematic of trolls: they are shifting and changing, hard to pin down in the end, except perhaps by what they are not: human, normal, helpful. The troll on the tram line in Oslo may have helped my friend to solidify her emerging Norwegian identity, but it also made the wind die down, froze her to the spot and left her fascinated but frightened.

Old Norse prose also attests the verb *trylla*, which is derived from the noun troll and which we might for the moment translate as 'turn (someone or something) into a troll'; the more general translation is 'enchant'. A large percentage of the recorded usage of this verb focuses on appearance: changed, non-human or both. A standard dictionary of Old Norse provides these passages (I translate the forms of the verb *trylla* with 'entroll').

> Large and much entrolled, so that he was a shape-shifter.
> They carried out rites and entrolled him such that he was like no other man.
> And afterwards he was entrolled and turned into a snake.

The interesting question here is what is primary: the transformation itself (he was a shape shifter), or the end product (unnatural; snake). Since the verb is derived from the noun, language history might favour the second option, but the question is complicated by the modern mainland Scandinavian languages, in which the prefix *troll-* (Danish *trold-*) usually means 'magic'; thus, for example, Mozart's *Zauberflöte* ('Magic Flute') is *Trollflöjtan* in Swedish. But just when we think that magic may be primary, we must consider other modern evidence: in Icelandic, *trylla* (my 'entroll') now means 'drive insane', and *troll-* as prefix means 'giant'. I think we have to accept that there has always been a considerable range to the semantics of the troll family of words, and that there have been different developments in the different language areas. Thus etymology tells us what we already know: trolls are not good. And they keep bad company. A late Icelandic saga, bordering on fairy tale, tells of Núdús, the king of Serkland (the Baghdad caliphate):

> He is larger and stronger than every other man and beyond each in every way in that part of the world. He has with himself all kinds of peoples, Africans and trolls and berserks and giants and dwarfs and other people powerful in magic. No human person can stand up to him and his army.

Around 1200 an anonymous poet, possibly from the Orkneys, compiled a poem with a series of proverbial sentiments. One stanza includes the following couplet, which rhymes in the original:

> All exaggerations seem short;
> not much is worse than trolls.

That sentiment probably still holds, at least with respect to trolls. They are still important, and they still have the power to invoke in us negative feelings like those of the poet who composed this verse so long ago. When he invoked trolls, everyone who heard or read his poem knew exactly what he was talking about. Anyone who reads this verse today will also have an immediate idea of what he had in mind, a powerful image of the part of our world that we just cannot explain. Trolls have been around for 1,000 years, and they are not going away.

I

The Earliest Trolls

Trolls enter the literary record in verses attributed to Viking Age poets, but even at this first moment they are challenging and striking. We first hear *from* a troll rather than hearing *of* trolls. The troll in question has a verse exchange with Bragi the Old, the first named poet in the North, credited with the creation of the verse form that Viking Age poets and their descendants in Iceland used for centuries. This Bragi appears in many sources, including a tenth-century poem describing the entry of the vanquished king Eiríkr Bloodax into Valhǫll (Walhalla), the abode of the Nordic gods; Óðinn (Odin), the head of the gods, is gathering up heroes for the last battle against the forces of chaos and evil, and Bragi stands alongside these heroes. A few centuries later, medieval antiquarians appear to have lost sight of the distinction between these heroes and the gods themselves, and they conceived of Bragi as a god of poetry. It is therefore significant that he was the first person to meet a troll. We do not know much about the human poet Bragi, but he appears to have been active in the late ninth century in Norway. From our point of view, then, the first troll appeared in a late ninth-century forest in Norway, and she revealed herself to a poet.

The exchange is recorded only much later, *c.* 1220–30, in the medieval Icelandic poet and statesman Snorri Sturluson's book *Edda* (the title probably means 'poetics'). It is found in the longest section of the book *Skáldskaparmál* (Poetic Diction) and was probably cited because it had many expressions for denoting a poet, as it did for designating a troll. Sturluson tells the story succinctly, as a legend narrator would. Here are the relevant passages in Anthony Faulke's translation (1995):

Bragi the Old spoke as follows when he was driving through a certain forest late in the evening; then a troll woman accosted him in verse and asked him who was going there.

The troll speaks first:

Trolls call me moon of the dwelling-Rungnir, giant's wealth-sucker, storm-sun's bale, seeress's friendly companion, guardian of corpse-fjord, swallower of heaven wheel; what is a troll other than that?

Bragi responds:

Poets call me Vidur's [Odin's] thought-smith, getter of Gaut's [Odin's] gift, lack-nought hero, server of Ygg's [Odin's] ale, song-making Modi, skilled smith of rhyme; what is a poet other than that?

The first line of each verse might also be construed as 'they call me a troll/poet'; this semantic uncertainty does not, however, change our understanding of what trolls or poets might be called. Before turning to the verses, let us consider the situation. Bragi is driving through a forest, either with a wagon or a sled. By its very nature this forest is at some distance from human habitation, perhaps a considerable distance (otherwise Bragi might be walking rather than driving). We do not know what the troll woman is doing there, but the fact that she challenges Bragi suggests that he has entered her domain. Humans rule their own dwellings and the areas they use and cultivate around them; the rest is mysterious and the domain of Other beings. It is late at night, and therefore likely to be dark, or at best semi-dark if the encounter takes place in summer. The perceptual situation thus fits the model of empirical supernatural experience described in the Introduction.

We do not know what this first troll looked like. There is no indication that she was larger (or smaller) than Bragi, and no indication that she was old or young, beautiful or hideous, or just ordinary-looking. If it was truly dark, Bragi may only have heard rather than seen her. We the readers know that she is a troll woman. In the scene we are reading, Bragi may have learned that she was a troll only by hearing her verse.

Each of the two verses in this exchange consists of a list of the kind of metaphor we call kennings in Old Norse poetry. In these a base word that has nothing to do with what the poet is thinking of is modified by another word to indicate the meaning. Thus Modi is a son of Thor, but a Modi who makes songs is a poet. Modi in the mythology is no such thing, and the kenning would work just as well with the name of any other god, or hero, who was not a poet. Frequently these kennings are unintelligible without knowledge of myth and heroic legend. With this background, we can attempt to examine what the troll claims other trolls call her.

Unfortunately, this first troll spoke enigmatically. The only clear kenning of her speech is 'swallower of heaven wheel': that is, 'of the sun or moon'. In the mythology, at Ragnarök, the end of the world, a wolf is to swallow the sun or moon (the word used can mean either). This is of course a cosmic threat. If there is no sun, there is no daylight. Crops fail, there is no fodder for animals and humans die. If there is no moon, humans cannot reckon time properly. While this may sound less disastrous than starving in the dark, time-reckoning was established in the mythology early on by the gods, and in human life time-reckoning was tied to crops and fodder in that it told people when to plant and when to harvest. Sun or moon, the threat is cosmic. This cosmic threat is probably also taken up in the first and third kennings, although not without slight changes to what the manuscripts actually say. If those changes are accepted, the troll invokes the name 'Rungnir [giant, destroyer] of the dwelling of the moon [the sky]' and 'bale of the storm-hall [the sky]'.

In addition, the troll woman is a 'wealth-sucker', and even if we do not know how that term should relate to a giant it sounds bad, and is probably an attack on human prosperity, since it would be possible to construe 'wealth of the giant' as a kenning for gold. She is the friendly companion of a seeress and guardian of the 'corpse-fiord' (graveyard), indicating connection with chthonic forces and the dead (according to the mythology, some seeresses may in fact be raised from the dead). So: trolls represent a threat to the cosmos, are destroyers of prosperity and are associated with death. This is not a reassuring resumé.

Bragi responds with ways to refer to a poet. Three of his kennings invoke Odin, head of the gods and a real god of poetry: Odin's thought, his gift and his ale (in the mythology, poetry is made material in mead, and Odin brings it to gods and men). In addition, Bragi's verse employs more rhymes and other flourishes, and it seems clear that he wins the exchange. The poetry of humans is thus more powerful than the poetry of the trolls, and in fact we hear only a few verses from any supernatural beings in the extant record, but thousands from humans.

There is a small footnote to this argument, however. The last section of Snorri's *Edda* is the *Háttatal* (Enumeration of Metres), a praise poem Snorri composed for the young Hákon Hákonarson, king of Norway, and his guardian, the jarl Skuli. The poem, which is embedded in a metrical commentary, comprises 102 stanzas, each exemplifying some metre or aspect of diction. Snorri calls one of the metres *trollsháttr* ('troll's metre'). This comes toward the end of the second section of the poem and is followed by what appears to be 'ghost's metre', then 'mouth-throwing' ('improvisation') and finally 'formless' (earlier there is also a 'witch-metre'). Troll's metre is rather stately, a variation of a basic form that was to prove popular with Christian poets as the Middle Ages progressed. I can see nothing in it to connect it with trolls.

The exchange between Bragi and the troll woman forms a paradigm that will often recur: a threatening encounter, in a place far from human habitation, between troll and human, with the human emerging unscathed in the end. The characteristics of threat to the cosmos and to humans and their prosperity, and the association with death, are assigned to the female in this encounter, and indeed Old Norse literature and mythology have a clearly gendered system in which the female is associated with disorder and darkness. Not all trolls are female, but it is perhaps instructive that this first one is. For the rest of their history, trolls continue to be associated with disorder and darkness, with the non-human, with chaos and the Other. Here Snorri's *Edda* gives us yet another piece of information. Some of the manuscripts contain versified lists that have come to be called *þulur*. Although they may not be original to Snorri's work, they do rely on knowledge of poetical (and thus mythological and heroic) traditions. Among these are five stanzas containing more than 60 names of troll women. Some of these we recognize, but most we do not. Some, however, are transparent in meaning, such as Bakrauf ('rear-hole', or anus), Harðgreip ('hard-grip') and Loðinfingra ('shaggy-fingers'). Interestingly, there are no *þulur* for male trolls, only for giants (*jötnar*), and no *þulur* for female giants. Poets seem, then, to have thought of the word troll as more appropriately attached to female than to male monsters, and it is poets who give us the earliest information about trolls.

Perhaps the most beautiful poem of the Icelandic Middle Ages is *Völuspá* (Seeress's Prophecy), which appears to make use of Christian as well as pre-Christian imagery in its powerful portrayal of the origin and ultimate demise of the cosmos. It is likely to be the creation of an Icelandic poet working around the time of the Conversion (*c.* 1000 CE). The three kennings of Bragi's troll woman setting forth a cosmic threat presage this verse (translated by Carolynne Larrington; 1996), set in a terrifying sequence of visions of the unravelling world.

> In the east sat an old woman in Iron Wood
> and nurtured there offspring of Fenrir;
> a certain one of them in the form of a troll
> will be the snatcher of the moon.

In the mythology, Fenrir is a son of Loki, friend and enemy of the gods. Apparently born a giant, he has sworn a blood-brother oath with Odin, the chief god, and is 'numbered among the gods'. When the gods perceive that this son of Loki poses a threat, they transform him into a wolf, and then bind him. In the process, Fenrir chews off the hand of the god Týr, and at the final battle of Ragnarök he swallows Odin. He remains in wolf form throughout. Because Old Norse inflects for gender, we know that this wolf who will snatch or swallow the moon (or sun) in troll form is also male.

When Fenrir's lupine descendant snatches or swallows the moon (or sun – again, the word can mean either), he will be in the form of a troll. Snorri may offer a hint about what the poet meant by this expression. In his description of Ragnarök in the *Edda*, he wrote this about the wolf Fenrir, who has broken the bonds the gods put on him:

But Fenriswolf will go with mouth agape and its upper jaw will be against the sky and its lower one against the earth. It would gape wider if there was room. Flames will burn from its eyes and nostrils.

If we connect this statement with 'the form of the troll' in *Vǫluspá*, we may well have in that poem the first indication that trolls could appear as large, misshapen and truly frightening beings. Also important is the implication that trolls can be involved with the changing of shape, guise or skin. Furthermore, wolves are wild animals, and they threaten domestic beasts and occasionally even humans. Like Bragi's troll woman, they inhabit the woods and other places far from human homes, although they do sometimes invade the domestic space of humans. We should therefore associate trolls with the wild rather than the domestic or tame; with outside rather than inside; with nature rather than culture.

Snorri Sturluson quotes another early use of the word *troll*, this time in his compilation of sagas about Norwegian kings called *Heimskringla* (Orb of the Earth). In the first saga of the compilation, *Ynglinga saga* (Saga of the Ynglings), Snorri quotes extensively from the poem *Ynglingatal* (Enumeration of the Ynglings), attributed to Þjóðólfr of Hvinir, another early Norwegian poet, perhaps even Bragi's contemporary. The poem comprises a catalogue of the earliest Swedish kings, focusing on the ways in which they died. The first stanzas deal with prehistory and approach myth. Stanza 3 contains the word *trollkund*, a feminine adjective meaning 'troll-related, of the family of trolls'. The verse, which is full of difficulties, is shown here in a literal translation:

But to visit
the brother of Vili
the creature of magic
arranged for Vanlandi,
when the troll-related night-Hildr [witch]

was to tread underfoot
the enemy
of the band of men;
and that necklace-destroyer [king],
whom the nightmare strangled,
burned on the bed of Skúta.

Snorri cites the verse in connection with the following story, which can be summarized thus:

The Swedish king Vanlandi visited the Finn Snær the Old and married his daughter, Drífa. The following spring he returned to Uppsala and failed to keep a promise to return to Drífa within three years. After ten years, she arranged for a woman with magic powers [Old Norse *seiðkona*, a woman who practices *seiðr*, a kind of shamanic magic] to charm Vanlandi back to Finland or kill him. When shortly thereafter Vanlandi found himself eager to return to Finland, his retainers dissuaded him from the trip. He was then attacked by a nightmare – not a bad dream, but a supernatural being, more often female than not, who disturbed men and animals in their sleep. When Vanlandi's men protected his head, she attacked his legs, and when they protected his legs, she attacked his head and killed him. He was cremated by the banks of the river Skúta, and his son with Drífa succeeded him as king.

In Snorri's understanding of the verse, the 'troll-related witch' was both a Finn and a sorceress. In Old Norse, *Finn* can refer both to Finns and to the Sámi people, but in either case, the witch was an ethnic outsider. It is certainly possible that she was also the nightmare who killed Vanlandi and was therefore not only a shape-shifter (transforming from a witch into a supernatural being) but also one who could act invisibly. The nature of trolls as ethnic outsiders and as shape-shifters with certain magic powers would remain salient for centuries.

Like Bragi, most humans in later legends about nightmares walk away intact from their encounters. The fate of Vanlandi, however, shows us that threats from the trolls and those related to them are serious, despite what happens in most texts. Thus there is always a tension when humans meet trolls, for although the odds favour the human, the trolls do win from time to time.

Another poet who wove trolls into his verse was Kormákr Ögmundarson, the eponymous protagonist of *Kormáks saga*, one of the subcategory of Sagas of Icelanders we call skald sagas. Kormákr lived in tenth-century Iceland. In one of his verses, Kormákr stated that a fair woman (his beloved Steingerðr, according to the prose context) gave his ring to the trolls, which seems to be a way of saying that she threw it away. In another, he says that trolls have done something to a woman, perhaps trampled or enchanted her. Finally, the saga writer attributes a verse to Kormákr's adversary Holmgöngu-Bersi in which Bersi says: 'May the trolls take me if I never again redden my sword with blood.'

These three verses share a characteristic use of the plural. According to this usage, the trolls are conceived as collective beings, like other creatures in the folk belief attested in Old Norse: *landvættir* ('land spirits'), *dísir* (collective female spirits related to fate) and so forth. All these collective beings are associated with the Other: the mysterious, inexplicable and unknowable. If one throws something away, it goes among the trolls. It becomes invisible and presumably never returns to the world of human beings. The same fate may befall humans, which leads to the proverb 'May the trolls take him/her/them/me/you'. Holmgöngu-Bersi comes down to us as the first to utter a version of this proverb, but he was hardly the last.

In its poetic context, at least, this proverb seems to mean 'to die'. An anonymous verse retained in *Haralds saga hárfagra*, the saga of Harald Fairhair (ruled Norway *c.* 860–930 CE) in Snorri's *Heimskringla*, made this brief report on an encounter in the Orkneys between the Norwegian Torf-Einarr Rögnvaldsson and two Vikings named Tréskeggr and Skurfa. If it is genuine (and we can never be sure), it would have been composed *c.* 900.

Then he gave Tréskeggr to the trolls,
[and] Torf-Einarr killed Skurfa.

Another example also involves two Vikings, but here they are poets. Somehow, according to *Grettis saga*, one of the classic Sagas of Icelanders, the Hebridean Vikings Vígbjóðr and Vestmarr extemporized and spoke simultaneously this little verse, just before a battle with a fleet led by, among others, Önundr Ófeigsson, known as Tréfótr ('pegleg'), because he had lost a leg in a previous battle.

> May the trolls have all of Tréfótr,
> may the trolls cast down all of them.

The trolls had Vígbjóðr instead. His sword became stuck in a wooden block Önundr was supporting himself with, and when Vígbjóðr bent down to retrieve it, Öndundr hacked off his arm. The wound was fatal.

Although scholars are fairly sure that the verse of the Hebridean Vikings does not go back beyond the time of the composition of the saga centuries after the battle (and how, indeed, could they have simultaneously extemporized a verse?), it is tempting to contemplate connecting the proverb with not just any death, but specifically with violent death. Such a connection has further support. This we find in the 'death-song' attributed to Ásbjörn prúði ('gallant') Virfilsson in *Orms þáttr Stórólfssonar* (The Tale of Ormr Stórólfsson). *Orms þáttr* dates perhaps from the later thirteenth century and shows a curious mixture of characteristics, including one unmistakably postclassical feature (although many readers will think it classically 'Viking'): Ásbjörn dies when his captor slices open his belly, attaches one end of his long intestine to an iron pole and makes him walk in a circle, thus winding his intestine around it. Ásbjörn nevertheless manages to compose and recite nine more stanzas, in the third of which he expresses his certainty of death:

> Now, betrayed in faith,
> I will explore the dwellings of the trolls.

Ásbjörn called the land of the dead 'the dwellings of the trolls'. The circumstances in which trolls lived, and indeed their entire world, became the subject of speculation in later Old Norse literature and folklore but were left untouched in these early texts. In them, inter-action between trolls and humans always occurred in the world of humans, as it did for my acquaintance in Oslo in 1973. Thus the troll-related witch came from distant Finland to kill King Vanlandi in Uppsala, and we can infer something similar from a verse composed in the later eleventh century by Þjóðólfr Arnórsson in his *Sexstefja* (Poem Equipped with Six Refrains), an elaborately crafted encomium praising the Norwegian king Harald Harðráði ('hardrule') after his death in 1066. In the twentieth of 35 extant stanzas, Þjóðólfr refers to a rebellion that the king had suppressed in the years before his death. He announces that peasants had kept Harald from enforcing law and that people had behaved badly, but that trolls had broken brushwood into the shoes of the enemies of the king who were responsible for these indiscretions. The expression 'break brushwood into shoes' is difficult, and most scholars are inclined to understand it as something like 'prevent their progress, so cause trouble generally'. If this reading is correct, then 'trolls' probably means supernatural beings in general, and indeed ones loyal to the land, like the *landvættir*. This suggests variation in terminology, and in fact such was precisely the case.

Indeed, according to the German scholar Katja Schulz, 'troll' is the most used term for giant, and it is also used synonymously with the word for those giants who oppose the gods in mythology. The main word for them is *jötnar*, which is of uncertain etymology but which came to mean giant (that is, very large creature) in the modern Scandinavian languages. The giants of mythology are not particularly large, or at least no larger than the gods. They are first and foremost the group with whom the gods compete for resources. Like the trolls we have considered thus far, they live not in the centre but at the peripheries. They threaten the gods in all sorts of ways but almost never carry out their threats. The exception is Ragnarök (the end of the world), but there the giants/*jötnar* win at best a pyrrhic victory. Like the gods, they all die in the final battle, and then the cosmos is destroyed. But when a new cosmos arises, it is peopled by offspring of the gods, and of course humans, but no giants are mentioned. If this new cosmos is the one in which real people were conceived to have lived during the Middle Ages and later, the trolls will have taken the place of the giants. Or to put it another way, as the giants are to the gods in the mythology, so trolls are to humans.

We have already seen that Fenrir's size at Ragnarök was cosmically large, and down on earth, too, trolls could be enormous. As far as I know, the first really huge troll was sighted during the Settlement period in Iceland (*c.* 870–939). It is recorded in one version of *Landnámabók* (Book of Settlements), which chronicles the settling of the island. A man named Lón-Einarr was running for his life along the southern coast of the Snæfellsness peninsula from an ambush by a neighbour whose wife he had accused of witchcraft, when he saw a *tröllkarl* ('old troll man'). This creature was sitting atop the cliffs named Drangar 'and was rocking his feet back and forth, so that they touched the surf, and he crashed them together to make spray'. These two cliffs, volcanic plugs now known as Lóndrangar, are 75 and 61 metres tall, so his perch may have been a bit uneven. Even if he was sitting only on the shorter one, and even if his legs did not reach all the way into the sea, this old troll man would have been around 100 metres tall.

As if that were not enough, the troll went on to declaim a verse (he is one of the handful of troll poets we know of, other than the troll that Bragi met in the woods). Pursued and pursuer paid the verse no heed. Today we find it nearly impossible to understand, with the exception of one clause: 'No giant makes more boats wet than I do'. Since there is plenty of fishing from the small beaches in the coves along this coast, and fishing boats are launched from directly below the cliffs, I think that the troll man is boasting about his ability to threaten men at sea, to disrupt their fishing and thus the livelihood of the community. In this he is a typical troll.

Indeed this troll was gigantic, but what is interesting here is the idea that in the verse he calls himself a *jötunn*, which, as we have seen, is the main word for 'giant'. This reaffirms that *troll* could denote 'giant', but it also shows that *giant* could denote 'troll'. Indeed, other words within this semantic field could both be denoted by *troll* and could denote 'troll'. Some of these other words mean 'giant', but it is surely significant that there is a set of words that denote female monsters: giants or trolls (*gýgr, flagð, gífr, fála*). Once again we see the female equated with the threatening Other.

It is important to stress that while some trolls could be huge, there was no requirement for great size. In the mythology, as I have said, there is scant indication that giants and trolls were larger than the gods (or that gods were larger than humans). One exception was Hrungnir, whom Thor overcame in a duel. Hrungnir was so large that when he fell dead, his leg pinned Thor beneath him. Thor's precocious three-year-old son lifted the heavy leg. Hrungnir also had a heart and head made of stone, so he was no ordinary giant.

Snorri Sturluson mentions more than once in his *Edda* that Thor, the great enemy of the giants, travelled to the East to fight trolls. These could as easily be giants. In the imagined world of the mythology, east and north are the bad directions. North as a dangerous direction makes sense anywhere in Scandinavia; east makes sense in Norway, since going east from the coast will quickly put you in the mountains.

Probably no more than large size accounts for the nicknames *troll*, given to one Norwegian around 1200, Arnbjörn troll, and *trolli*, which apparently one Norwegian and one Greenlander bore.

Old Norse attests an adjective, *troll-aukinn*, which should mean something like 'made large by trolls'. Although one true giant does rate this adjective, he is just one of many giants (*Þorsteins þáttr bæjarmagns*). The most interesting person to bear this adjective is Þorleifr Þjóstolfsson, who according to *Landnámabók* was one of the early settlers near Patréksfjörður in southern Iceland. His family put their faith in St Columba, although they were not baptized, and of Þorleifr one manuscript says that he was greatly *troll-aukinn*, but converted to Christianity. Here something other than size is surely meant.

We can see this in some other extended or metaphorical uses of *troll*. Thus in *Egils saga*, when the famous eponymous saga hero Egill Skallagrímsson arrives unexpectedly at the hall of his friend Arinbjörn after having been shipwrecked on the coast of Northumbria, the servant who answers the door and conveys the name of the caller to Arinbjörn inside adds that the man at the door is 'as big as a troll'. Years after his death, Egill's bones were disinterred; they were much larger, heavier and thicker than those of other men, especially his skull. The priest Skapti Þórarinsson took Egill's skull, and placed it on the churchyard wall. The skull was wondrously large, but what seemed even more amazing was its weight. All the outside of the skull was wavy, like the shell of a large mussel. Skapti decided then to investigate the thickness of the skull, and so he took a very large hand axe and raised it with one hand as strongly as possible and struck the skull with the hammer and wished to break it, but where the blow struck it only turned white and neither broke nor burst. From that one may conclude that this skull was not easily harmed by the blows of lesser men, when a sword and flesh accompanied it.

This skull sounds a bit like Hrungnir's stone skull, and it could certainly have contributed to the notion that there was something troll-like about Egill. The saga tells us that at the age of three, Egill was as big as most boys of six, and at twelve he was as big and strong as most grown men. Just as important, in my view, is that at the age of seven he murdered an older boy who had beaten him in a wrestling match. So trolls could surely be thought of as large. Indeed, Katja Schulz has estimated that the word *troll* in the Sagas of Icelanders refers to a giant about 35 per cent of the time. In the legendary sagas, a genre we will consider in the next chapter, the percentage is higher, some 55 per cent. But there is more going on with Egill than just size. Yes, he is as big as a troll, but his numerous destructive and anti-social acts (there are many in the saga, and at this point the reader has encountered most of them) also make apt a comparison with trolls.

The luckless Grettir of *Grettis saga* was also a huge man. Once in a storm he swam from a ship across an inlet in Norway to get a flame. When he entered the house, people took him for a troll, and in the ensuing struggle the house caught fire and burned down. While this was not a deliberately anti-social act, the aftermath of Grettir's actions was no better than what might have occurred had a real troll visited the house that night.

Another human with troll-like stature was Helgi, the half-witted son of Ingjaldr, with whom the outlaw Gísli takes shelter in *Gísla saga Súrssonar*. We read that Helgi was the greatest fool and a half-wit; that consideration was granted to him, that a stone was tied about his neck, and he grazed outside as did the cattle and was called Ingjaldr's fool. He was very large in stature, almost like a troll.

Later in the saga Gísli tricks his enemies by pretending to be the boy. He is on a boat with a servant woman when they approach. He says to the servant woman: 'Tell them that the fool is aboard, and I'll sit in the bow and imitate him and twist myself in the fishing lines and sometimes be over the side and act as crazily as I can.' Gísli must have been somewhat similar in stature to Helgi, and both were presumably large men. Beyond that, however, it seems most likely to me that the boy's behaviour also marked him out as a troll, just as I have argued that Egill's did. Egill was anti-social and destructive; Helgi was asocial and without speech, bound to graze like a household animal. This opens up another aspect to trolls: sometimes they are stupid or dim-witted. Some folk tales turn on this idea, but in older Scandinavian literature and folklore trolls are certainly never clever.

What could be more anti-social than the living dead? *Eyrbyggja saga* also tells of the revenant Þórólfr bægifótr ('Lame-leg'), whose grave men opened in order to destroy the corpse. 'He was still not decomposed and was the most troll-like in appearance; he was black as Hel and thick as a bull.' Hel was a daughter of Loki who presided over a world of the dead. Beyond this culturally specific detail, however, Þórólfr looks like many revenants (those who return from the dead) and his physical attributes are like those of werewolves and vampires in many traditions. These attributes have much to do with the actual physical appearance of the human body after death; among the most important of the processes of decomposition are discoloration and swelling. It is hardly coincidental that such changes make the once human but now somehow different shape of Þórólfr into something 'the most troll-like'. The frequent link of trolls and the dead may therefore have to do with actual natural processes.

In what followed his disinterment, Þórólfr managed to pass along in the form of rebirth something of his 'troll-like' attributes. Men burned the corpse and the ashes flew off and were later licked by a cow. The cow disappeared for a time and was said to have been seen in the company of an otherwise unknown dapple-grey bull. She gave birth to a calf, also dapple-grey, which was later named Glæsir. A blind woman with second sight heard the calf howl and said: 'That is the sound of a troll, and not of any living being, and please kill that evil thing.' The calf was spared, however, and grew to be an enormous bull. Later the blind woman heard it bellow, and said: 'The troll was not killed, and we will get more trouble from it than words can express.' She shivered whenever it bellowed and finally predicted in a verse that Glæsir would kill her foster son Þóroddr, the master of the farm. With age the bull became increasingly large and intractable, until finally it began tearing up the home field. Þóroddr attacked it with a heavy wooden post, and they struggled for some time before Glæsir succeeded in fatally goring Þóroddr. Thereafter it ran off to a bog and threw itself in, and that area is now called 'Glæsir's spring'.

Glæsir is, according to the blind woman with second sight, a troll, even though it never has human form (but it does have a name). It has links with the human troll Þórólfr, or more accurately with Þórólfr's corpse (a revenant) and hence with the world of the dead, and its links with the otherworld are established by its mother's lengthy stay away from the farm, her dallying with an unknown dapple-grey bull (dapple-grey has strong connections with the supernatural) and by throwing itself into the bog, away from human habitation. Indeed, the connection lives on in the name 'Glæsir's spring' for a natural feature of the wilderness.

The story continues, and it opens up views of magic that are crucial to understanding the nature of some of these earliest trolls. The daughter of Þórólfr bægifótr, the revenant who was burned, was Geirríðr. She was a woman with famous supernatural powers and indeed was sued, unsuccessfully, for using her spells to attack a young man so viciously that he lay wounded all winter. It was said that she had, like a nightmare (remember Vanlandi!) ridden him. As the feud develops, another female with supernatural powers, Katla, has been using magic spells to hide her son from Geirríðr's supporters. Geirríðr puts on a coloured cloak – always a danger signal in the sagas – and sets out towards Katla's farm. When Katla sees someone approaching in a coloured cloak, she says: 'That will be Geirríðr the troll, and deluding-spells alone will not suffice.' Geirríðr's magic is more powerful than Katla's, and the son is found and bound. Before she is put to death, Katla confesses that it was she whose attack caused Geirríðr to be sued.

An incident similar in its equation of magic and trolls is preserved in *Landnámabók*. Steinrøðr the Powerful is the son of a settler and has cured people from attacks of evil creatures. Once he comes unawares on the witch Geirhildr, who changes herself into a leather bag full of water. Steinrøðr is a smith and has an iron staff with him, which he uses to beat the disguised Geirhildr. An anonymous verse describes their encounter, and it includes the line 'the troll's ribs are swollen'.

The characteristics of these early trolls would persist. Trolls are still dangerous and anti-social, associated with peripheries rather than centres, sometimes easily spotted, sometimes not. As the following chapters will show, trolls lived easily in the human imagination.

2

Medieval Trolls

I n the previous chapter I mentioned that trolls were not known as poets in Old Norse tradition, although a few did leave some verse. Probably the most interesting of them turns up in a short narrative found in a late fourteenth-century manuscript. We call this text *Bergbúa þáttr* (The Tale of the Mountain-dweller), and most scholars accept that it was written down in its current form by someone in a monastery. It tells of an otherwise unknown man named Þórðr in western Iceland who sets off to church one winter night on some high holy day, taking an unnamed servant with him. Caught in a blizzard, they hide in a cave, where they hear twelve stanzas in the complex metre called *dróttkvætt*, repeated three times during the course of the night; the last stanza urges them to learn it. In the morning they continue to the church but have missed the service. On their way home, they find no cave where they think it should be. The protagonist subsequently moves his homestead closer to the church. He has learned the poem, and he prospers, but the servant does not learn it, and he dies within a year.

The whole thing sounds a lot like the model of empirical supernatural experience we took up at the beginning of this book. The men are under stress, both from the storm and from the fact that they are spending the night in a cave and will miss the church service they set out to attend. Although they first hear noises in the cave, the releasing stimulus is visual:

> Then they saw what looked like two full moons or large shields, and the distance between them was not so small.

They were sure it was two eyes and that he who had such lanterns would not have a narrow face.

This big fellow refers to himself in one of the verses as a 'rock-elf', a kenning easily construed as 'troll'. However, this troll, although large, does not overtly threaten the humans, except through his admonition to learn the poem. The tale thus enforces the value of oral tradition: to learn and to transmit verse – that is, to participate in the oral tradition that encoded knowledge – is to live; to fail to do so is to die. And because Þórðr has marked the cave's entrance with a cross and trusted himself to God while he listens to the poem, it also confers God's grace on the act of hearing and learning it, whatever its content. And the content does sound somewhat questionable from a medieval Christian perspective. The first stanzas tell of a volcanic eruption, with loss of life, and the later stanzas focus on the pagan god Thor, apparently presenting him not only as an enemy of men (a traditional Christian view) but of giants (a pre-Christian view).

It is not impossible that the stanzas tell of a specific volcanic eruption, the so-called Hallmundarhraun in Borgarförður. It could have taken place *c.* 940–50, which would make it the first major eruption in Icelandic historical time: that is, the first that the Icelanders experienced. Interestingly, *Landnámabók*, the Icelandic 'Book of Settlements', reports that a settler went up to a cave in that area, around that time, and recited a poem for a giant who lived in it. We could imagine this giant as an ancestor of our troll, the first to put the poem into circulation among the monsters of the wilderness, who kept it there until Þórðr rescued it for us.

Insofar as shape-shifting is fundamental to the notion of trolls, the term might conceivably be extended to cover nearly any being of the otherworld, as we have seen. It might also, in time, come to be used of beings who have more to do with imagination than with the believable. We meet examples of trolls like this in medieval Iceland, alongside the more or less believable trolls surveyed in the previous chapter. Here is one of them, the troll Gríðr in *Illuga saga Gríðarfóstra*, a product of the late medieval (perhaps fifteenth-century) Icelandic imagination. Illugi, the modest human protagonist (there is also a prince in this story), has entered Gríðr's cave in search of fire, when he hears her heavy footsteps as she returns to the cave:

> He thought a storm or squall was blowing out of her nostrils. Mucus was hanging down in front of her mouth. She had a beard but her head was bald. Her hands were like the claws of an eagle, but both arms were singed, and the baggy shirt she was wearing reached no lower than her loins in back but all the way to her toes in front. Her eyes were green and her forehead broad; her ears fell widely. No one would call her pretty.

What I find most striking about this description is the blurring of categories: male/female (beard and bald head), animal/human (claws), immodest/chaste (her garment). Such blurring suggests powerful operation of the imagination in creating the degree of otherness as it plays with the very shiftiness of trolls. Given this level of imagination, the litotes of the summary sentence is stylistically striking.

Gríðr has, however, a beautiful daughter whom she offers to Illugi if he can say three true things. This he does:

> Your cave is tall and wide; I've never seen a bigger or stronger building. Your nose is so big that I've never seen a greater monster than you, and it's so dark that the floor is beautiful when compared with you, and I've never seen anything more wretched than you. Your daughter is certainly better looking, and I've noticed the greatest difference between you two, and so would everyone say who saw you both.

It turns out that Gríðr is actually Signý, daughter of the king of Álfheimar ('elf-land'). Her wicked stepmother turned her into a troll, and she must kill every man who goes to bed with her daughter, until one displays no fear. That one turns out to Illugi, and he frees Signý/Gríðr and her daughter from the spell. Illugi marries the daughter. King Sigurðr, Illugi's silent partner, marries Signý, but not before Gríðr (it is the author who switches between the two names, not I) has killed the king's evil counsellor, Björn, who had called the daughter a troll woman. Those were apparently fighting words.

Many other extravagantly described trolls fill the pages of the later Icelandic legendary sagas. They appear to be distant indeed from the believable trolls, but there exists a connection, in the way that appearances and reality change or can be changed when magic is applied. For example, one troll causes the catch of Ketill Hængr ('trout') to vanish every morning: he steals it at night. Later Ketill enters into a poetic exchange with a troll woman, described in a simile (a rare trope in Old Norse literature) as 'black as pitch'. When he intends to shoot his arrows at her, she utters a chant against them, changes herself into a whale and dives under the surface, all to no avail. His arrow hits its mark, just beneath her fin.

Even when the trolls are hardly believable, the trio of size, strength and magic serves to make a troll, or to make a man like a troll. The language is practically formulaic. Each of the following examples comes from *Göngu-Hrólfs* saga, and they are repeated in other sagas.

> The greatest troll, both in strength and size.
> The greatest troll in his magic.
> The greatest troll on account of size and power.
> More like trolls than men because of his power and size.

The leader of a group of Vikings in *Hrólfs saga Gautrekssonar* is said to be huge and terrible to look at, touching on the usual formulas, but then the author adds that not only are this man and his band impervious to weapons, they also eat everything uncooked and drink blood. Thus they are more trolls than men. *Karlamagnús saga*, the Norse adaptation of the *Chanson de Roland* and other *chansons de geste*, ascribes to Burnament a similar appetite, and makes an interesting lexical comment:

> He eats only raw food and drinks no wine unless it is mixed with blood, has yellow eyes like those of a cat but could see more clearly at night. This man was full of magic and sorcery and fraud and would be called a troll if he were to come up here to the northern part of the world.

So, in the medieval Scandinavian imagination, trolls were still local, even if similar beings existed elsewhere.

The native sagas, too, go in for exaggeration of the physical characteristics of trolls. In another late saga, *Gríms saga loðinkinna*, Ketill's son Grímr is captured by a female of unbelievable ugliness: no taller than a seven-year-old girl, but so stout that Grímr doubted he could get his arms around her; she was long and hard of face, bent-nosed and bare-shouldered, swarthy and gaunt-cheeked, foul of appearance and bald in front. Her hair and skull were both black, and she wore a shrivelled skin cloak. When the author informs us that she is barely kissable because of the mucus dripping from her nose, we suspect immediately that Grímr will have to kiss her, and so he does. Later he gets into bed with her, but he falls asleep immediately. When he awakens, he sees his beautiful fiancée beside him. At the foot of the bed is the garment that made her ugly: a 'troll woman skin'. Her stepmother had transformed her into this ugly creature and Grímr has met the conditions for releasing her from the curse.

These two examples of stepmother-induced troll form fit, of course, into the broader story pattern of the loathly lady, as in Chaucer's 'Wife of Bath's Tale' and the many analogues to it that scholars have adduced. We should certainly also think of the spells in fairy tales that turn princesses into cats and swans (and princes into frogs and wyverns). What is significant in the Icelandic case therefore is that the troll was so readily available to fit this slot of the beautiful princess turned temporarily ugly, and that it offered authors and storytellers the opportunity to embellish the loathsomeness of the form of the enchanted lady.

Not all such trolls are female. Here is a troll couple encountered by the hero Arrow-Oddr:

> They saw that trolls were sitting on both benches. A villain sat there in the high seat, huge and terrible. He had a lot of hair, black as the fan-like pitches of whalebone, with an ugly nose and eyes. A woman sat on one side of him; to describe the one is to describe the other.

Hálfdan Brönufóstri ('foster-relative of Brana'), the protagonist of an eponymous saga probably from the fourteenth century, met a troll couple in a cave. He had been shipwrecked in an unknown land, which he later tells his men he thinks might be Helluland ('Slab-land'). What is interesting about that is that Helluland is one of the three place names associated with North America in the two so-called Vinland sagas, which offer the textual evidence for Norse presence in North America later supported by archaeological evidence, principally at L'Anse aux Meadows in northern Newfoundland. Today most scholars identify Helluland as the rocky shores of Baffin Island, so I suppose we might say that Iron-nose and Sledge-hammer (I have translated their names, which are transparent in the original) are the first North American trolls. Hálfdan has gone up into the glacier hunting, and on a path he finds footsteps that are four ells (about 2 metres) apart. He follows the track.

> There he saw a big cave and a bright fire in it. He goes up
> to the cave door and sees that two trolls are sitting by the
> fire, one female, the other male, and the cookpot was between
> them. In it was the meat of both horses and men. The man
> had a hook in his nose and the woman a ring. They played
> a game in which he hooked the ring with his hook, and both
> ends were up [in the air], but when the hook slipped out of
> the ring, the old lady fell over backwards. She said then: 'I
> don't want to play this game, my darling Iron-nose.' 'As you
> wish, dear Sledge-hammer', and they lifted the top off the
> cookpot. Then Iron-nose spoke up: 'Sledge-hammer, is there
> anything left of those twenty-five men I enchanted up here
> last winter?'

This scene of domestic bliss is interrupted when, as Sledge-hammer returns with the last two men left in the pantry, Hálfdan beheads Iron-nose. In the ensuing battle with Sledge-hammer, they wrestle inside, then out near a gorge, until Hálfdan succeeds in beheading Sledge-hammer, not, apparently, without some unseen help.

We may have an analogue here with Beowulf's battles first with Grendel and then Grendel's mother. In any case, once again the female troll seems to be the more dangerous, not just because she is the second troll, but because the battle with her is much more difficult.

Hálfdan's unseen helper in the fight with Sledge-hammer was Brana. She had a giant father and a human mother. She too grew up in a cave, and Hálfdan and his men help her kill her father. A lot about this rings of trolls, but the author never uses the word. Interestingly, however, Hálfdan himself was the son of a half-troll (the offspring of a marriage between a troll and a human). That lineage does not seem to resonate in the plot, except to give Hálfdan (whose name literally means 'half-Dane') the special birth that fairy-tale heroes often have. Or it may explain the affinity between the son of a half-troll and the female half-giant who 'fosters' him, or in this case becomes his protector and sometime lover.

Another person of mixed lineage is Högni in *Þiðreks saga* (the saga of Dietrich of Bern), the product of the union between a human woman and a king who later reveals himself to be an elf. At the age of four he can beat up the other boys and he looks like a troll. Specifically, his face is as pale as bast and as wan as ashes but large, frightening and fierce. Since in Old Norse light colours are associated with elves, 'troll' here probably has a general rather than specific sense.

Högni is a king's son, and although trolls typically live off in the wilderness, in caves or the like, they were sometimes imagined to have social organization like that of humans. Not long after Ketill Hængr killed the troll woman who had changed herself into a whale, he met another troll woman, this one with a mane hanging down to her shoulders. He asked her where she was going:

> She drew herself up opposite him and said: 'I am going to the troll-assembly. Skelkingr, the king of the trolls, is coming there from the north in Dumbshafr, and Ófóti from Ófótans-fjord, and Þorgerðr Hörga-troll, and other great creatures from up north.'

The name Skelkingr is related to words meaning 'mock/mockery', and his home territory, Dumbshfr, is the 'misty sea', probably the Arctic Ocean north of Norway (it appears in other texts, even though

Skelkingr does not). Ófóti, which looks as though it should mean
'Un-foot', is found as the name of a giant. Manuscript variation and
other evidence indicates that Þorgerðr Hörga-troll is identical to
Þorgerðr Hölga-brúðr ('bride of Hölgi': possibly her father, in an
incestuous relationship that might typify trolls), a supernatural being
(goddess? monster?) associated with the notoriously pagan Jarl Hákon
of Hlaðir (Trøndelag), who preceded the missionary king Olaf
Tryggvason (995–1000) as ruler of Norway. According to one story,
Jarl Hákon sacrificed his son to this Þorgerðr when a battle was
going badly. A huge hailstorm arose, and those with second sight
could see Þorgerðr shooting arrows out of her fingertips, and so the
tide of battle turned. In one version of the story, the leader of those
being attacked says: 'It seems to me that we must do battle today
not with men but with the worst trolls' (he uses the plural because
Þorgerðr is accompanied by another woman). Þorgerðr was no doubt
large; the so-called First Grammarian, who treated Icelandic phonology
as early as 1175 or so, made one of his points by citing this sentence:
'A tall [woman] died when Hölga-troll died.' Þorgerðr must have
been well known.

Did people appreciate this kind of tale? We have evidence from
a more or less contemporary account. Sturla Þórðarson, nephew of
Iceland's most famous medieval writer, Snorri Sturluson, ventured
to the Norwegian court in 1263 to present a poem he had composed
in praise of King Hákon Hákonarson, in order to bring about
reconciliation. Hákon had already left for a military campaign to the
Hebrides, where he died, and Hákon's son Magnús was ruling the
court when Sturla arrived. They meet on ships in a harbour, and the
reception is chilly. At night a member of the king's crew asks if
anyone wants to provide entertainment, and when no one volunteers,
he turns to Sturla. Sturla then tells what the text calls *Huldar saga*
('the saga of Huld'): not a text we still have because, of course, it was
performed orally. Sturla tells it skilfully, and the queen hears the
commotion.

The queen asked, 'What's that crowd up forward on the
deck-planks?' The man says, 'People want to hear the saga
that the Icelander is telling.' She said, 'What saga is that?'

'It's about a huge troll woman and it's a good saga and well told.'

Magnús urges his queen to ignore it and go to sleep, but the next day she summons Sturla and asks him to bring (that is, be prepared to tell) the troll-woman saga he had been telling last night. He complies. The king's anger seems to abate somewhat as the day progresses (it was clearly a long saga), and when it is over Sturla wishes to recite his poem. The queen urges the king to give him leave, and finally Sturla agrees. The poem works its wonder: Magnús even thinks that the recital outdoes that of the pope, and Sturla joins Magnús's court. Magnús later even commissions him to write his father's and his own biography. We know Sturla today as this biographer, as the author of sagas about contemporary Icelandic history, as a lawman and as a poet.

We also find trolls in the language of the laws, which were written down between the twelfth and fourteenth centuries. The Norwegian laws have a famous provision in a section about such crimes as oathbreaking and rape, against 'sitting outside to awaken trolls in order to perform heathenism', and it is found in other laws as well. Although this expression could just mean calling up devils, it surely also relates to native conceptions.

We could think of these trolls as the moving dead, or as some other kind of made monster, of the sort often called 'sendings' in Old Norse and Icelandic tradition, because people with magic powers send them out malevolently against other people. In the medieval Norwegian context, we might also think of helping spirits called up by Sámi *noaiddit* ('shamans'). The medieval *Historia Norwegiae* tells of two Sámi shamans, one of whom is killed by the spirit of another. Should we think of that spirit as a troll? In Latin the shamans are called *magi*, as we might expect, but the helping spirits are *gandi* (singular *gandus*), which is a borrowing from Old Norse *gandr* 'something enchanted; sorcerer's tool'. The magical nature certainly suggests trolls.

The Gulaþing law (from the area around Bergen) had a provision against vicious slander, such as claiming that a man has borne children, or been anally penetrated by another man, or calling him a mare, bitch or whore. The penalties for such speech aggression were severe. Also actionable, and to the same degree, was calling a man a troll or a witch, or a free man a slave. Given the collocation with witches and slaves, I am disinclined to think that what is at issue here is calling a man a demon. Probably troll has the sense of one who works magic but in this instance it clearly refers to one with no status and nothing to contribute to society.

The Borgarþing law (from around the Oslo fjord) had a very interesting provision making clear the connection between trolls and witches. This provision begins by outlawing 'sitting out', and engaging in 'Finn-journeys' (shamanic journeys undertaken by Sámi people) or prophecy. The meat of the provision has to do with witchcraft. It ends by discussing the situation of a woman who is *tryllsk* ('entrolled' according to my rendering; otherwise usually 'enchanted'). She needs the oaths of witnesses (these are what we would call character witnesses), and if she cannot obtain a sufficient number, she must leave the district. She can, however, take her property with her, 'because she herself is not the cause of her being a troll'.

In general in the laws from Norway and beyond, the concept of the troll is associated with witchcraft. A troll woman is a witch, and a 'troll-rider' is a nightmare, like the one who rode Vanlandi centuries before the laws were recorded. The word trolldom is frequently recorded for magic, the kind that is not permitted under Christian law.

Calling a man a troll has fatal consequences in one Icelandic saga, *Finnboga saga ramma* (The Saga of Finnbogi the Strong). Finnbogi is a historical character, but much of the saga involves wholly fantastic adventures that take place outside Iceland. The episode in question, however, takes place after he has returned. His two sons, aged five and three, like to amuse themselves by teasing a cantankerous old neighbour who is rumoured to be a shape-shifter. Once they call him a troll, 'even though you look like a man', and he kills them. Finnbogi takes immediate vengeance in what he later says was the hardest battle of his life.

Troll-riding – or trolls troubling people – also exists outside the laws. In the saga of Guðmundr, bishop of the northern Icelandic diocese of Hólar in the early thirteenth century, we read of a certain man, Snorri, who was persistently beset by a troll woman (she is also

called a *flagð*, or 'witch'). One Saturday night he must travel alone
to Mass, and the troll woman forces him off into the mountains. He
calls upon Guðmundr (already something of a local saint), and a
great light appears. The troll vanishes, as if sunk into the ground,
and the light leads Snorri to safety.

The vanishing troll has analogues in a feature most of us associate
with trolls: they are in trouble if the sun touches them. While bursting
was to become common in later folklore, in the Middle Ages turning
to stone was more common. This happens once to a dwarf whom Thor
keeps asking questions and, more importantly for our purposes, once
to an ogress. This incident occurs in the anonymous medieval Icelandic
Eddic poem 'Helgakviða Hjörvarðssonar' (The Poem of Helgi, Son of
Hjörvarðr; trans. Carolynne Larrington, 1996), and here too the monster
stays up too late because of a dialogue. She is talking with Atli, one of
the hero Helgi's men. She starts the dialogue by challenging Atli to
identify his king. Atli responds, and the dialogue ensues:

> 'Helgi is his name, and you can never
> bring harm to the prince;
> there are iron plates on the prince's ships,
> no troll women can attack us.'
> 'What is your name (said Hrimgerd), mighty warrior,
> what do men call you?
> The prince trusts you, since he lets you watch
> in the pleasant prow of the ship.'
> 'Atli I'm called, atrocious I shall be to you,
> I am most hostile to ogresses;
> I've often stayed at the dew-washed prow
> and tormented night-riding witches.
> What is your name, corpse-greedy hag?
> Troll woman, name your father!
> You ought to be nine leagues underground
> with fir-trees growing from your breast!'

In the translation cited above, Carolyne Larrington has, quite rightly
in my view, used 'troll woman' for the Old Norse *fála*, a fairly rare
noun whose etymology has to do with deception.

The dialogue goes on for a while, and then it is all over:

> Look east now, Hrimgerd! Since Helgi has struck you
> with fatal runes,
> both on land and sea the prince's ships are safe
> and so are the prince's men.
> It's day now, Hrimgerd, Atli has kept you talking
> until you laid down your life;
> as a harbour-mark you look ridiculous,
> there transformed into stone.

Commentators have noticed that as a navigational aid, the ex-troll is not harmful but helpful to mariners, the very people she has been threatening. A later Faroese ballad has St Olaf turn a giant into a stone and tell him that he will now mark a landing place.

In seeking to take Snorri into the mountain, the troll woman in the saga of Guðmundr the Good anticipates the action of trolls in later folklore. But in hindering Snorri from reaching church, she shows the religious thinking that was able to incorporate trolls. In Icelandic literature about the conversion of Iceland, trolls were demonized. The *Óláfs saga Tryggvasonar in mesta* (Great Saga of Olaf Tryggvason), from the Icelandic fourteenth century, has an instructive example. Olaf ruled Norway 995–1000, and in the sagas of Norwegian kings he usually plays the role of the first missionary king, although this record had to be adjusted a bit to accommodate the later Olaf Haraldsson who died in 1030 to become St Olaf and thus was also regarded as a missionary king. Olaf Tryggvason replaced Jarl Hákon as ruler of Norway and, as was mentioned above, Hákon had the reputation of an enthusiastic pagan. On a trip down the coast, Olaf's men learn that the district Naumedal is so beset with trolls that people can hardly live there. Two of Olaf's retainers sneak ashore one dark night and come upon a meeting of trolls, sitting by a fire outside the mouth of the cave. The troll who appears to be in charge asks the others if there is anything to the story that Olaf Tryggvason has come to the district and may make trouble for the trolls. So he has, according to the trolls who respond (also in the narrative called fiends and unclean spirits). One troll reports that he was maiming Olaf's men by squeezing them, but when he tried it on Olaf, Olaf squeezed back, and the troll cried out at the burning pain. A second says that he tried to serve poison to Olaf at a banquet, but that Olaf poured the poison over the troll and then clocked him with the empty horn. A third says that he changed himself into the form of a beautiful woman and slipped into Olaf's bedroom and was going to kill the king when he fell asleep, but that Olaf whacked him on the head with a book (presumably a prayer book) so hard that his head has been crooked ever since. Although this scene clearly has to do with demonization, in the troll with the crooked head we see echoes of trolls with twisted and lumpy bodies.

This demonization could carry over into more fantastic literature too. *Þiðreks saga* (The Saga of Dietrich von Bern) has a long section about Vélent (Wayland the Smith). He comes to an island, fells a huge tree, hollows it out and moves into it. A Danish king (Niðuðr) comes to the island and orders his men to start chopping the mighty fallen trunk. When they realize that there is a man inside, they assume that it must be the devil himself. Vélent emerges and says to the king: 'I'm a man, Sire, and not a troll.' Later in the saga, the knight Vildifer emerges from a bearskin disguise, and the author tells us that men realized that he was not a troll but a man.

The collective trolls we saw in the proverbial expressions in the previous chapter that equate the world of trolls with dying recur in some of the later materials. Once we find a woman reporting that her parents have died of old age and been buried, or 'given to the trolls'. Most frequently attested, however, are curses, such as 'May the trolls take you!' A more forceful example is the outburst of Bergljót, the wife of the Norwegian noble Einarr Þambarskelfr ('jelly-belly') in *Halldórs þáttr Snorrasonar* (The Tale of Halldórr Snorrason), a text associated with the sagas of King Óláfr Tryggvasonar and perhaps written down in monastic circles in Iceland in the late twelfth or early thirteenth century. Einarr had taken in the Icelander Halldórr, who frequently entertained Bergljót with his storytelling. When an evil young relative of Einarr recited a slanderous verse about Halldórr, she replied: 'It is wicked to assail men unknown to you with calumny and slander, and trolls will tear your tongue out of your head. Halldórr has proved himself in his wisdom to be beyond most other men in

Norway.' What Bergljót meant is perhaps that the slanderer would die, and Halldórr indeed kills him after an additional insult. The trolls here remind us of medieval devils, meting out appropriate punishment in hell, as would be appropriate for a text written first by and for monks. In any case, Bergljót's words have a proverbial ring, and the words troll, tear and tongue are linked by alliteration in Icelandic too: *ok munu yðr troll toga tungu ór höfði.* Indeed, the expression is sometimes altered in a more churchly direction, in which the trolls get not the body of the dead person but his soul.

In at least one instance, it seems that there may be an ethnic component to the use of the word troll. This is found in *Grænlands annáll* (The Annal of Greenland), a medieval Icelandic account of what was going on in Greenland. One of the main figures in the later period is Björn Einarsson, famous as a pilgrim to the Holy Land. But he also went up to Greenland towards the end of the fourteenth century and stayed there for some time, for he prospered there. The annal attributes this prosperity in part to interaction with trolls:

And finally it helped most, that he rescued two trolls, a young brother and sister, from a skerry. They swore him an oath of allegiance, and he did not lack provisions after that, since they took care of procuring all the meat or fish he desired or needed. To the female troll it seemed that most had been granted to her when her mistress Ólöf allowed her to touch and play with her new-born son. She also coveted her mistress's headpiece and decked herself out with whale guts. They killed themselves, jumping into the sea from a mountain behind the ship on which they were not permitted to sail, when their beloved master Björn returned to Iceland.

Now, these could be garden-variety trolls, but the Inuit in Greenland were of course extremely skilled at extracting food from the Greenlandic seas and landscape and to use just about every part of every kind of animal they caught. There is also a cliché about Greenlanders' fondness for children. As an ethnic Other group, the Inuit might well have been called trolls. *Flóamanna saga*, one of the so-called Sagas of Icelanders, has some Icelanders journey to Greenland. According to one manuscript, they see some 'troll women' (this could mean female trolls, or also witches) near a stranded whale on the beach, and the leader of the Icelanders hacks off the hand of one of these women and thus procures the whale for the Icelandic party. In a parallel manuscript, the victims are described as two women in skin jackets, presumably a reference to the anoraks worn by Greenlanders. These passages suggest that in medieval Iceland the term troll might well have been used to describe ethnic Others in a far-off land to which few travelled but which really did exist.

The medieval literature of Denmark and Sweden consists of translated material to a much greater extent than that of Iceland and Norway. When, therefore, trolls appear, there is often an underlying Latin original to testify to the translator's notions. Among the Latin originals are *bestia* ('beast'), *demonum* ('demon') and *monstrum* ('monster').

The Old Swedish story of the mother of St Bartholomew ('the woman without hands') gives a fanciful description of a troll: 'His handless wife has given birth to a troll most like a devil, which has a large head, crooked neck, clumsy hands and feet, donkey ears, terrifying eyes.' Not infrequently, people are human in the upper parts of their bodies and trolls (*bestia*) in the lower. One such example is in *Konung Alexander*, the Old Swedish translation of Walter of Châtillion's twelfth-century life of Alexander the Great, *Alexandreis*. Interestingly, in the poem this luckless devil is 'in the form of a troll', echoing the words of the seeress who sang about the wolf who swallowed the sun in the form of a troll.

The poet of *Konung Alexander* also mentions dragons with troll form. Alexander and his men have come to a spring and have drunk from the sweet water there:

> Then came dragons in the form of trolls
> many and large and very fierce
> they flew out from mountains high
> in the water they wished to bathe
> and they wished too to slake their thirst.
> Many a warrior they would awaken
> with their eyes that spew poison.

Their breath was like hot flame,
and whoever received that breath,
he was instantly as good as dead.
Their mouths stood ever open,
burned as red as live embers.
Their breasts rose up in the heights,
so rigid that no one could bend them,
they also carried in their heads,
each of them, one spike or more,
worse than any horn of an animal.
They stop before no wall.
The earth shook from the storm
that accompanied that flock.
From their wings went din and clamour.

The Swedish poet is mostly paraphrasing here; where he has 'dragons in the form of trolls' the Latin has *serpentes et dragones*, 'serpents and dragons'. While the word picture would fit serpents and dragons, the native *troll* must have brought the concept a bit closer to home. Later in the poem a woman in Babylon gives birth to a son also said to be 'in the form of the troll'. This unfortunate lad is human above and troll below.

One translator used 'trolls and devils' for the *idola* ('idols') that pagan men serve. A translator of Bonaventure wrote: 'They thought they saw phantasms, that is, something that seems other than it is, as it is said that people see trolls or conceal virtue.' In this latter case we have a third view of trolls. It stands alongside the believable trolls of folk belief and the fantastic trolls of literature: these are things that do not, indeed cannot, exist in God's order of the world. They are always something other than what they seem to be; when people see trolls, they are actually seeing something else. This, of course, is what folklorists came to believe in the twentieth century, although from a secular rather than sacral point of view.

In this incorporation with Christian literature, trolls side with Satan, and their ethical status is clear. We should, I think, take seriously the dualistic world view this kind of classification implies: on the one hand trolls, devils, magic, the dead and the uncontrolled supernatural; on the other humans, angels, the empirical world, the living and controlled encounters with the sacral (as in church) or the supernatural (as in miracles). This distinction helps clarify the all too close connection between trolls and the dead, which might lead to the erroneous assumption that trolls are nothing more than the dead. Such reasoning would draw on the reports in Icelandic sagas that people could 'die into the mountain' (Helgafell, on the Snæfellsnes peninsula just south of the village Stykkisholmur, is the best example) and would connect them with mountains as the abode of trolls. And indeed, they inhabited the same sphere. But so did devils and the damned in hell.

Two or more Other species can comfortably inhabit the same space, so long as they are distinguished along some meaningful axis. The dead are quasi-human non-living Other, while trolls are non-human non-dead Other. What is fuzzy about this distinction is in fact subsumed in the fuzzy application of the word troll for all sorts of other beings.

As demons, trolls were naturally overcome by holy men and saints, as we saw above with St Olaf and the trolls in Norway. In Lund, Sweden, we can actually see what may be a troll in the crypt of the cathedral. Built as the cathedral for the archdiocese of all Scandinavia (when Lund was part of Denmark) and consecrated in 1123, the structure has of course been altered over time, but the crypt is thought to date from the inception of the cathedral. In it are numerous piers, among them one of a figure clutching the pillar and near it a woman. As early as 1593, a visitor noted these figures in his diary and added that people thought they were giants opposed to building the church on that spot. Not quite 60 years later, in his *Encomion regni daniæ*, Jens Lauritzon Wolf recorded the first version of the legend that has become attached to these figures. St Lawrence, the Roman deacon whose cult maintains that he was roasted on a gridiron, and to whom the cathedral was dedicated, is here in what was then Denmark, trying to hurry along the building:

It is said that a troll came to him and offered to finished the church quickly, with the condition that St Lawrence was to address the troll by name; if he could not do that, he was to

The 'Giant Finn' pier in the crypt of Lund Cathedral.

give him the sun and moon, and if St Lawrence could not do that, then the troll was to poke out St Lawrence's eyes, and St Lawrence agreed to that, too. But what happened? The troll took no rest and built the church quickly, and when St Lawrence saw that, he was greatly downcast ...

In great sorrow St Lawrence went out of Lund and was wandering, and from wandering and oppressive thoughts he became tired and weary, and eventually he lay down beside a mound to rest. And while he was resting he heard the troll's troll-children howling and weeping, at which the mother, who was inside the mound, spoke to one of the children thus: 'Be still, my son, your father Find [Finn] will come and bring you the sun and moon to play with, or both of St Lawrence's eyes ...'

The troll stopped before St Lawrence and demanded his payment and wages for his work, to which St Lawrence responded: 'Believe me, Find, I will give you no payment until the church is finished.' When the troll heard that word, Find, with which St Lawrence had named him by name, then he grew so angry and ferocious that he grabbed a pillar with both arms and wanted to pull down the entire church, which St Lawrence forbad him through the power of Him who is greater and more powerful than the troll. After that the troll and troll-wife and children remained at the pillars, where they may be seen today.

Indeed, more than 300 years after these words were printed, one can still see them. While it is possible that the carver intended to carve Samson or a stone-mason, or some unnamed monster, and that the male and female figures may have nothing to do with each other, it is clear that they were associated with this widespread legend centuries ago. Similar legends were told of many churches in Scandinavia, with different heroes (in Norway usually St Olaf, for other churches just some unnamed minister). Sometimes the master builder is called a giant, sometimes a troll, sometimes nothing. But he is troll-like in that he (or his family at least) lives in a mound and, more to the point, that he threatens not just a holy man, but the entire cosmos.

It is perhaps no surprise that a largely parallel story is to be found in Scandinavian mythology. At the advice of Loki, the gods commission a master builder to build a wall around Valhöll within a year, and the payment is to be the sun, moon and the goddess Freyja. With the help of his horse, the builder nearly completes the wall, and Loki is on the spot. He changes himself into a mare and lures away the horse, and the builder, like Find, flies into a giant rage, thus indicating his affiliation. Thor kills him, and later Loki-as-mare bears a foal, the eight-legged horse Sleipnir. Although the name of the master builder is thus not an issue, his identity is, and the outcome – his death – is not uncommon in the legends either: often the builder is just setting the spire when the hero calls out his name and he plummets to his death.

There were other trolls who worked hard. Although it may be stretching the definition of 'medieval' to mention a work from 1555, trolls would have no objection to stretching the truth, so neither do I. The work in question is Olaus Magnus's *Historia de gentibus septentrionalibus* (History of the Nordic Peoples). Olaus (1490–c. 1558) was in ecclesiastical service and was appointed bishop of Uppsala in 1544, an entirely symbolic act since the Reformation had already taken place and Olaus was in exile in Rome. He is famous for his map of the North as well as for the *Historia*. The latter work contains a great deal of what we would now call social history and even ethnography. Book VI is devoted to mines, and it contains a short chapter about demons in the mines:

Demons make great efforts to perform services for the inhabitants of these parts, most often, however, in stables and cowsheds and in the mines, where they break up, hollow out, and split the rocks, which they load into skips or buckets, and carefully fit the little wheels and pulleys by means of which the hoisting gear operates. As and when they please, they show themselves to the miners as shadowy shapes in all possible forms; with the sound of voices they counterfeit laughter and senseless roars of merriment, and they play frolicsome tricks and countless other jokes, with which they deceive the poor men. But they actually turn their simulated

Olaus Magnus, a mine troll (or mine demon), illustration from
Historia de gentibus septentrionalibus (1555).

compliance into calamity, and finally into death, by shattering
props, or they destroy or rout the miners through a fall of rock.

Since Olaus goes on to quote a German authority on such matters,
and since it is unlikely that he visited a Swedish mine, we may be
doubtful, but later folklore does put supernatural beings in mines.
They are not called trolls (the usual term is *gruvrå*, or 'mine-spirit')
but are classified as trolls, as we shall see in the next chapter. Indeed,
when in the early twentieth century Olaus Magnus's *Historia* was
finally translated into Swedish, these demons were called *bergtroll*,
or 'mountain trolls'.

Olaus's *Historia* was equipped with numerous illustrations, and
one of these shows the mine demon/troll.

In chapter Five we will meet a Swedish poet's fanciful description
of mine trolls. But first we will take a look at trolls, believable and
not so believable, in and from folklore.

3

Folklore Trolls

As noted above, the collection of folklore from oral traditions began sporadically during the Reformation in Scandinavia. It culminated in the nineteenth and early twentieth centuries and continues to the present day. Given the enormous chronological and geographic spread, it is difficult to generalize about any aspect of Scandinavian folklore, including trolls, but it would be fair to say that the semantics encountered while examining the earlier conceptions characterize more recent traditions as well. The term 'troll' seems to have become almost an all-purpose word for supernatural beings who may be large or small, solitary or social, real or imagined. The connection with magic remained strong and is exemplified semantically: the verb *trolla/trylla* means to enchant or carry out magic. As a prefix, *troll-* usually has the same meaning. Above I mentioned *Trollflöjten*, the magic flute. This object works for good in the opera, and when we see that Gandalf the Wizard is called *trollmannen* ('the troll-man') in the Norwegian translation of Tolkien's *The Lord of the Rings*, we must certainly dismiss the notion that all trolls are monstrous. Still, the word frequently does have a negative connotation. In Danish, Shakespeare's *Taming of the Shrew* is 'taming of the troll', and standard Norwegian *trollet* (literally 'entrolled, bewitched'), the past participle of the cognate of Old Norse *trylla* and dialect *trollslig* ('troll-like'), means 'naughty'. Many compounds in initial *troll-*, particularly in the rural dialects, refer to features of the natural environment. A dragonfly may be a *trollslända* in Swedish (the standard term is just *slända*), and a tufted duck is a *troldande* (literally 'troll-duck') in Danish. Norwegian *trollbær* (literally 'troll-berry') is a baneberry (*Actaea spicata*); *trolldruva* ('troll-grape') in Swedish. *Trollhegg* ('troll-hedge') is buckthorn (*Rhanmus*), and *trollkrabbe* ('troll-crab') is a lithodes crab (*Lithodes maja*). A *trollgryte* ('troll cookpot') is a pothole, and *trollmjøl* ('troll-flour') is calcium cyanide, used as a fertilizer or weed killer. Perhaps most interestingly, Norwegian *trollkjerringspytt* (literally 'troll woman's or witch's vomit') may refer to several kinds of algae, mould or insect saliva; the entry in Haugen's dictionary notes that all were 'thought to be vomit of a witch's cat'. Many Swedish dialect terms suggest such reasoning: *trollspy* ('troll vomit') is a kind of algae; *trollspott* ('troll saliva') is the white substance surrounding the larva of an insect as it sits on a blade of grass; *trollsmör* ('troll butter') is a kind of yellow mushroom; and *tunn troll* ('thin troll') is a mould that grows on wet substances. This list hardly exhausts the possibilities, but it demonstrates the principle of attaching trolls semantically with the unexplained or Other part of the environment. Whence, otherwise, came these algae or moulds, which grew seemingly out of nowhere and sprang up almost overnight? What better explanation than fluids from a troll associated closely with and almost blending into the landscape, like the one my friend saw in Oslo?

Within folklore scholarship, the wide connotations of the term 'troll' were recognized early. Andreras Faye, who in 1833 became the first to publish legends (oral traditional accounts of believable events) in Norway, noted the following in the preface to his edition: 'Jutuler ["giants"] and riser ["giants"] are in the legends often called trolls, which is to be regarded as a general term for all harmful supernatural beings.' Later he added: 'The biggest among them [the "underground people", another general term for supernatural beings], who are also called *thusser* or trolls, are as big as humans and live in ridges or mounds.' Juxtaposing these passages is instructive, for in the first, when he says that 'troll' is a general term, he uses *trold*. This is the Danish form, and in 1833, nineteen years after Norway had become a more or less autonomous part of the Swedish kingdom after four centuries under the Danish king, there was still no real written Norwegian standard. But when he writes about the biggest 'underground people', Faye uses a Norwegian form, *trølle*. This is something like me writing *trolls* for the general concept and, say, *tröll* for the specific modern Icelandic form.

Indeed, troll became a general term in Iceland. The first collection of Icelandic legends and tales was put together by Jón Árnason. He included a chapter on trolls, which he began as follows: 'The expressions "troll" and "troll woman" are quite comprehensive, because they denote all those beings who are greater than humans in some way and who are more or less ill-willed, for example, ghosts, or even wizards.' Nevertheless, he adds, the defining characteristic is large size.

The great nineteenth-century Swedish folklorist Gunnar Olof Hyltén-Cavallius witnessed the wide applicability of the term and, compared with Jón Árnason's view of the situation in Iceland, the variation. In his *Wärend och wirdarne* (Wärend and its Inhabitants), the most ambitious attempt at a Swedish ethnography, aimed at his home district, Hyltén-Cavallius wrote that the term *troll* came to be used for all sorts of supernatural beings, although in southernmost Sweden trolls were properly beings of small stature ('not larger than a "half-grown child"'), who lived far from human habitation and were not part of the Christian community. Later he added these words, suggesting continuity with the early and medieval trolls we have already met: 'The trolls could change their shape and take on any sort of form whatever, such as hollowed-out trees, stumps, animals, skeins of yarn, rolling balls, etc.' Most recent folklorists concur. Regarding terminology, Bengt Holbek and Iørn Piø, writing for a popular Danish audience, noted that not just the underground people, but all social nature beings, indeed, all the beings of legend, may be called trolls. Bengt af Klintberg reports that in Sweden, 'Popular tradition gives quite a contradictory picture of trolls' appearance. Sometimes they are described as dark and ugly, but from other data one can conclude that they essentially looked like human beings.' The high medieval ethical view lives on: 'What most clearly distinguishes trolls from humans is that trolls are outside the human community.'

The variety of possible meanings for the term troll in recent Scandinavian folk tradition was great. Texts recorded in the nineteenth and twentieth centuries display trolls as ordinary, large or small in stature, as fair and plain, enticing and stern, ordinary but misshapen, and one even as a cloudy wraith. Such variety is, of course, consistent with the notion of troll as a generic term for supernatural beings. Some trolls were age-old and helped form the landscape:

> In the old days there lived a troll in Børglum they called Skrolli. He took a few handfuls of dirt in his fists and patted them together and lived in the mound he had made in that way. But when he started carrying on in the district, people were sick of him, and they got some monks to move into the area, and people built a monastery for them by the side of the mound. Now Skrolli moved, for he couldn't bear the sound of their matins and the ringing of their bells. At the place where he had taken earth for his hill there were still some remnants of his work, and they are still there.

We can hardly doubt that his legend is set in the distant past; Denmark is hardly a place where monasteries are built willy-nilly. Skrolli is a troll, but he behaves like giants in legends: they lived long ago, helped to form the landscape (there are still remnants of his digging) and hate church bells. There are many legends telling of giants driven off by church bells, like Skrolli:

> In Holme at Århus a farmer's wife was standing one day in her door, when a little troll with a pointed humped back came up to her and said: 'Today Big Bjerg is marrying Little Bjerg. Will you be so good as to lend me a barrel of beer for a few days, if you get in return beer that is just as good?' Then the woman took the troll with her out to the brew house and said that he could take whichever barrel seemed the best to him. But since a cross had been marked on all the barrels, the troll couldn't take any of them. He just pointed and said, 'Off with the cross.' Now the woman understood that she had to remove the crosses, and when she had done so, the little troll put the biggest barrel up on his hump and went away with it. Three days later he brought back a barrel of beer, and that beer was just as good as what he had borrowed. From that day onward, good fortune came to that household.

Both this and the previous legend come from Jutland in Denmark. While the troll in the former legend was something of a giant who lived long ago, this one is a little misshapen neighbour. His size is part of a joke, since the couple whose wedding he is catering for are named Bjerg ('mountain'). Although the action took place some time ago ('From that day onward . . .'), there is nothing to mark it as in the very distant past. More generally, this text is of the sort that celebrates good relations between humans and supernatural beings. The human woman not only agrees to provide the troll with beer, but she effaces the crosses that made the beer off-limits to him. As a result of her willingness to be a good neighbour, she gets beer back that is equally good, but that is not the point. The point is that being on good terms with the supernatural beings can lead to good fortune. We may surmise that legends of this sort reinforced the notion of the benefits of being good neighbours.

There is probably another little joke associated with this legend, since it has the troll borrow and repay the beer. Trolls and other supernatural beings were notorious for stealing beer, entering people's houses in invisible forms and tapping a bit here and there and taking it off to their mounds.

Jonte in Skörhult was a man who saw more than others do. Once he was out threshing with my father, but a thunderstorm grew up, and then all the threshers gathered in a little crofter's cottage. Sure enough, lightning struck right down the chimney. Then a vent opened above the baking oven, and something black as a sack of coal rolled out. It was moving as though legs were kicking inside a sack. Then he rolled out through the door and took off down toward the lake, but then the lightning struck again, and then he just vanished. Jonte in Skörhult, however, saw that it was a troll. The lightning knocked off the troll's leg when it struck down the chimney and later killed him down by the lake.

Here it takes a person with second sight just to know that the formless black matter is a troll. Stories like this might support the idea that trolls are related, etymologically, to ball lightning, but the connection certainly seems slight.

More interesting is the connection with the pre-Christian god Thor. In the mythology, Thor is best known for his giant-slaying and, as we have seen, he is also said to kill trolls. In nineteenth-century Norway, folklorists were able to collect tales about Tor (Thor), *trollebane* ('troll-killer'). The etymology of Thor is 'thunderer', so the idea of killing trolls with lightning may be very old indeed.

In Stenkyrka cemetery a troll went out one night to haunt but left the hole into the grave open after itself. Along came a beggar through the cemetery, and he stuffed into the hole a loaf of bread he was carrying under his arm and then went into the sexton's to get lodgings for the night. He heard how the troll was carrying on out in the cemetery, for at the crow of the cock it couldn't get back into the grave. Now when in the morning the sexton went out to ring the church bells, the beggar accompanied him out into the churchyard, since they both heard the troll crying out. The sexton asked what could be carrying on so, but the beggar kept still. Now, however, he went back to the grave and took his bread out of the hole, and then they both caught sight of something like a cloud of smoke that was circulating around the hole and sank slowly down in the earth, and the hole closed after it. Then the beggar said that it was the troll, which could only now get down into the grave, after he had removed the bread. He said that he had seen the troll come up out of the hole in the same way, that is, as a cloud of smoke, but then immediately get grave clothes on and go out through a hole in the cemetery wall.

Technically, we would call the dead person who emerged as a wraith and went off in 'grave clothes' – that is, presumably – in human form, a revenant. For this storyteller, the term *troll* was suitable. Clearly s/he uses the term rather like an all-purpose word for something nasty and beyond the normal.

The folklorist Bengt af Klintberg has published an index of the types (recurring plots) of the Swedish folk legend. In it he devotes an entire section to what he calls legends about trolls and fairies. He distinguishes the two groups on the basis of where they live: trolls in mountains and hills, fairies in subterranean dwellings. *Fairies* is not, of course, a Swedish word, but af Klintberg uses it as a recognizable English term for certain Swedish words. *Troll,* on the other hand, is a Swedish word, although its plural is not *trolls.* Thus, af Klintberg is partly following the general tradition of using the word troll as a general term for supernatural beings, specifically those who live in mountains and hills. Although the word *troll* is actually used of the supernatural beings in many of the actual recordings, the index as a whole gives a summary of the kinds of stories in which trolls play a role.

Similarly, Lauri Simonsuuri used the German word *Bergtrolle* in his catalogue of Finnish belief legends, and when Marjatta Jauhiainen updated it and switched the language to English, she used 'mountain trolls'. The underlying Finnish is *vuorenpeikot*, from *vuori,* 'mountain', and *peikko,* 'hobgoblin, ogre'. Some Finnish–English dictionaries gloss *peikko* as 'troll'. Again, folklorists indicate that the word is internationally known.

Af Klintberg catalogues some 150 types, not including legends of changelings. He divides these into a number of categories: friendly coexistence; bread from the trolls; loans between trolls and humans; trolls and the sign of the cross; breach of norms activates trolls; celebrations and transportation among trolls; person can see invisible trolls; trolls suffer loss or damage; how to avoid being taken by trolls; taken into the troll mountain; released from troll mountain; trolls and thunder. These categories are meant to be descriptive, not analytic.

The legend I adduced above in connection with 'good relations' – the borrowing of beer – is typical of the category af Klintberg calls 'loans between trolls and humans'. Beer figures in many of the legends in this category, perhaps because it took advance planning to brew beer for an important holiday or event, or perhaps because there existed a certain ambivalence towards alcohol. Occasionally, instead of beer, porridge is the item borrowed, but in some legends it is instead a brewing tub or some other household tool. As if to indicate the reverse side of good relations, af Klintberg reports one rare type in which a woman lies to a troll who wants to borrow flour, beer and milk, claiming she has none. Her lies come true: after the troll leaves, the woman's larder is empty and her cows barren.

Af Klintberg isolates an entire category analogous to 'good relations', calling it 'friendly coexistence'. The loans of beer and other items would fit under this rubric, but as I have said, af Klintberg's aim is to break down the material into discrete descriptive categories. Into 'friendly coexistence' he primarily places legends in which trolls and humans help each other. Af Klintberg's first type, 'A journey with a troll', is probably best known internationally in the form given it by the nineteenth-century Norwegian folklorist Peter Christen Asbjørnsen. As we have seen with other early Scandinavian folklorists, Asbjørnsen seems to use troll as the general term, while the helper in this story is a *jutul* ('giant').

> Above the parsonage at Våge [now Vågå, in Oppland], there looms a pine-covered ridge or a small mountain with cracks and steep walls. It is Jutulsberg ['Jutul mountain'], to which Storm has dedicated a song. Through a trick of nature a doorway appears in one of the mountain's flat walls. If one stands on the bridge over the boisterous Finna river or on the meadows on the other side and looks at this doorway over the swaying garlands of the hanging birches and allows a bit of the power of imagination to help, it forms itself into a double door, coming together at the top into a pointed Gothic arch. Old white birches stand like columns on both sides, but their tops do not reach the beginning of the arch, and if the doorway reached in only the length of a church, Våge church could stand under the arch with its roof and tower. This is no ordinary door or gateway. It is the entrance to the jutul's palace. It is the 'Jutul's door', an enormous portal, which the biggest troll with fifteen heads could comfortably pass through without bending its neck. In the old days, when there was more contact between humans and trolls, if someone wanted to borrow something from the jutul, or to speak with him about other matters, the custom was to throw

a stone at the door and say, 'Open up, jutul!' [Asbjørnsen says he was there on a visit a few years ago, and he heard this story. He also saw many marks on the 'door' from stones being thrown at it.]

One of the last people to see the jutul was Johannes Sørigården from Blessom, the farm neighbouring the parsonage. But he probably wished he had not seen him. This Johannes Blessom [he takes the name of his farm] was down in Copenhagen for a lawsuit, since up here there were no courts in those days; and if one wanted to pursue a legal action, there was no other choice than to travel down there. This Blessom had done, and his son did the same after him too, for he also had a lawsuit. And so it was Christmas Eve. Johannes had spoken with the bigwigs and taken care of his business, and he was walking along the street somewhat downcast, for he longed to be at home. As he was walking, a fellow from Våge passed him in a white jacket with a leather bag and buttons like silver dollars. It was a big, tough-looking man. He thought he should recognize him too, but he was walking so quickly.

'You're walking fast, you are', said Johannes.

'Yes, I'm in a hurry', the man answered, 'for I'm going to Våge tonight.'

'Yes, if I could only go there too', said Johannes.

'You can ride behind me', said the man. 'I have a horse that runs twelve steps per mile.'

They went, and Blessom had his hands full just staying on the runners, for they went through storm and wind, and he could see neither earth nor sky. Once they landed and rested. Where they were, he could not tell, for they suddenly took off again, and he thought he saw a skull on a stake there. When they had come a while along the way, Johannes Blessom began to freeze.

'Oh no, I left my mitten there where we rested. Now my hand is freezing', he said.

'You'll just have to tough it out, Blessom', said the man, 'for now it isn't far to Vågå, and where we rested was half way'.

Before they got to the bridge over the Finna, the man stopped at Sandbuvollen and dropped Johannes off. 'Now you don't have far to get home', he said, 'and now you must promise me that you won't look back if you hear a noise or see a bright light.'

Johannes promised, and he thanked the man for the ride. The man went his way over the Finna bridge, and Johannes started up the hill to the farm at Blessom. But all of a sudden he heard a noise in Jutulsberg, and at once it grew so light on the road before him that he thought he could have picked up a needle. He didn't remember what he had promised, but he turned his head to see what it was. The jutul door was wide open, and it shone and gleamed out from it as if from thousands of candles. Right in the opening stood the jutul, and it was the man he had stood behind. But from that time on, Johannes Blessom's head sat crooked on his neck, and so it was as long as he lived.

Jutulsberg (the giant's door) was already famous in Norway, as Asbjørnsen indicates, through the 1775 poem 'Ode to Jutulsberg' by Edvard Storm, who was born in Vågå but had his career in Copenhagen. The poem celebrates Vågå and the surrounding nature.

Jutulporten ('the giant's door') has also become a tourist attraction. The website visitnorway.com has an entry on it in Norwegian, including this statement:

> In Presteberget ['Parson mountain', identical with 'Jutul mountain'] you will find the Jutulport, a large 'door' in the mountain. Inside lives the jutul with his wife. No one has seen the jutul since the time Johannes Blessom got a ride with him back from Copenhagen, but it is said that if you throw a stone against the door three times, he will come out. Why not try it? You never know!

It is worth noting that the *jutul* has been equipped with a wife, and that we now need to throw the stone three times, as in a fairy tale.

The English-language equivalent of this site simply tells the legend and adds some geological information. Those informed only by this website will not know to throw a stone at the door to invite the troll to emerge: perhaps he does not speak English? Indeed, although competent English is ubiquitous in contemporary Norway, the trolls would certainly be the last to remain stubbornly monolingual.

Although we do not know what the troll was doing in Copenhagen, it seems clear that he had concerns not dissimilar to those of Johannes Blessom. He does, however, appear to be wealthier than Blessom, having a fancy outfit and, especially, a horse and carriage. And his home in the mountain is well lit. On the one hand, the troll's offer to give Blessom a lift seems to have been inspired purely by generosity; perhaps we should infer that the troll saw how downcast Blessom was and wanted to cheer him up. On the other, if we are to admire the kindness of this troll, we must also consider that there was a skull on a stake at the place where he chose to rest (halfway between Copenhagen and Vågå could be imagined to be somewhere in the Oslo fjord, but I doubt if that is what Asbjørnsen or the storyteller had in mind). The troll was also somewhat bossy, telling Blessom to tough it out and then later not to look at the troll gateway. The line, 'You'll just have to tough it out, Blessom', has become proverbial in Norwegian, and you can still hear it and see it today, for example on chat boards. How many national languages have proverbs based on what a troll said?

The troll's interdiction ('don't look back') and its violation (Blessom looks back) and the consequence are very common in legends with trolls and other supernatural experiences. Dealing with trolls is always fraught with danger, and it is best to do as they say. Or to put it another way, the attitude towards trolls displayed in our recordings of the traditional rural culture is always ambivalent. Where there is help there may be harm, and where there is harm there may be help. It may help us to understand the *jutul* if we know that in some versions of this legend, the protagonist rides not with a troll or giant but with the devil.

Beyond a lift, troll help can take various forms. Perhaps most common is giving a hand with getting in the harvest, although sometimes trolls give advice about harvesting and brewing. Human help to trolls may involve fixing a tool, providing firewood or food for troll children, or lending a bridal outfit or table silver. In all these cases, we see neighbours helping one another.

In my view, af Klintberg's most important category is the one he calls 'breach of norms activates trolls'. This category relates to the model of empirical supernatural experience insofar as that model indicated that a breach of some norm could play into the psychophysical condition of an individual who sees a troll. Breaching of norms is also a powerful mechanism in stories. Af Klintberg calls one of the widely collected types in this category 'Borrowing the big kettle'. Reidar Thoralf Christiansen also catalogued it in his index of 'migratory legends' (international legends) based on Norwegian types; Christiansen called it 'Trolls resent a disturbance'. Here is a version from Halland, Sweden:

> In Veddinge there lived a farmer called Tore. He was often out late at night. Once he heard a troll in Koberg [a mountain] call to a troll in another mountain and ask to borrow the big kettle. 'What do you want with it?' the troll asked. 'I'm going to cook Tore's long bones, because he's out so late at night', answered the troll in Koberg. After that the farmer never dared go out in the evenings.

Presumably the trolls are troubled because the nights belong to them. But in other versions of the legend, the farmer is said to work late because of greed. Sometimes the focus is on farmhands who are forced to work late; the trolls threaten to cook their boss. And to make it clear that the trolls are enforcing norms, there are versions in which the person who is to be cooked is missing a church service or a feast-day such as Christmas.

The trolls, then, care what people do, and they take steps to correct errant behaviour such as greed, overworking labourers or missing church. One legend type indicates that trolls get fat on food cooked during the Sabbath, God's day, and others claim that trolls can get food when people curse, or fail to bless the food, or prepare food without washing their hands. So one reason that trolls exist (in people's imagination) is to ensure proper behaviour. The category 'trolls and the sign of the cross' shows how trolls cannot get their hands on food or other items over which humans have made the sign of the cross, and thus encourages good behaviour rather than discouraging bad.

Folklore tradition thus shows helpful trolls and trolls upholding human norms, albeit in frightening, threatening or downright harmful ways. But it also has trolls who threaten humans without any apparent motivation to uphold norms. The troll whom Bragi the poet met in the woods more than a millennium ago would fall into this category of malevolent troll, as would many – if not most – of the other medieval trolls. In the more recent folk legends of Scandinavia, trolls threatened or did all sorts of nasty things, of which the worst by far was 'taking into the mountain': in other words, kidnapping. We have already seen a thirteenth-century Icelandic version of this, in the story of Snorri taken up to the mountain by a troll and saved by a light when he appeals to Bishop Guðmundr. In more recent tradition, the trolls take the person *into* the mountain, rather than *on* it, but the principle is similar.

How the kidnapping occurs is difficult to say; in some legends we just learn that it has happened. Often the victim is alone, and sometimes out in unsettled areas such as the forest or the mountain. In such cases it is easy to imagine that kidnapping by trolls is used as an explanation for someone who went missing. Nowadays we would expect a missing hiker's remains to show up in due course, at the foot of a cliff, say, or when the snow melts, but identification frequently depends upon techniques of forensic anthropology that were unimaginable a century or two ago. If kidnapping by the trolls was used to explain the disappearance of people in the woods or mountains, we could perhaps say that trolls were part of a 'folk' science.

A small set of legends imagines a kidnapping from the very home of the person taken. In these cases, the trolls would sometimes place a wooden image of the person to be taken in her bed (it is usually a she). A common legend type involves someone hearing the trolls giving instructions on how to cut the wood: 'Make the feet big, like Tora's.' The kidnapping can then be averted. But in other cases, the husband sees what he thinks is his wife in bed, only to discover that she is gone and a block of wood is there in her place. Af Klintberg reports a legend from Skåne in southern Sweden in which the husband averts a kidnapping as the trolls are dragging his wife up the chimney.

As I have mentioned, although men and boys are kidnapped by trolls, most often the victims are women. In a study of kidnapping of humans by trolls, H. F. Feilberg reports that of the records available to him, kidnapped women outnumber boys and men by more than two to one. Women in childbirth are at special risk, as are new mothers who have not yet been churched (formal re-entry into the Church community after giving birth). During this period, normally six weeks, folk tradition regarded these women as not quite fully Christian and therefore vulnerable.

One way to undo a kidnapping was to take church bells near where the trolls live – this is usually also near the site of the kidnapping – and ring them (although not in Denmark, where the distances were usually small enough that moving the bells was unnecessary). Such a technique would also, of course, be useful if a person had not been taken into the mountain by the trolls but was simply wandering lost. Even so, there are a great many more narratives about unsuccessful than successful rescue attempts. Not infrequently it is the person's dead body that is recovered. And even when a rescue is successful, the person who has been taken into the mountain is never the same again. Some are sad and withdrawn, some are insane, some incapable of work; some, too, like Johannes Blessom, have permanent physical marks of their time with the trolls. Many legends, on the other hand, have a kidnapped person report to a member of the human community that her or his new life in the mountain is good, with good food and a high living standard. That would have been comforting to the family she or he left behind, and it ties in with the great wealth trolls in fairy tales keep in their castles. Still, proverbs make clear what the community was thinking. Two such proverbs were recorded as early as the seventeenth century, in Sweden's first collection of proverbs: 'Many a one takes a troll for gold' clearly warns against marrying for money. The other is even more explicit: 'The one who takes a troll for gold is left with the troll when the gold is gone.'

Besides kidnapping, trolls might overrun a farm, carrying on, eating, drinking and threatening humans. This they do most often at Christmas Eve. An alternative is overrunning a mill, and in the latter case they often burn it down on Christmas morning. Unlike kidnappings, these threats are almost always reversed. One common plot (one of the few to be classified by folklorists as both legend and fairy tale) has a visitor with a bear spend the night in the farmhouse that is to be overrun. The bear chases off the trolls, and when the trolls return next Christmas, they ask the man whether he still has his big cat. He tells them he does, and it has had kittens. This puts a permanent end to the problem. I incline towards thinking of this plot more as fairy tale than legend: that is, as less rather than more believable. The humour of the story lies in the inability of the trolls to distinguish between a bear and a cat, thereby confusing not just size, but the opposition of wild and domestic animals.

The trolls come at night. The night belongs to them, and they belong to the night. For this reason, they cannot abide daylight. The best illustration of this dichotomy is the motif of being turned to stone if caught in daylight, as witnessed in the last chapter. This conception lived on in Iceland. The Icelandic folklorist Jón Árnason even proposed a special subcategory of troll, 'night-trolls'. The stories he gathered under this rubric – and there are not a few – sometimes employ the word 'night-troll' for rock formations that legend tradition asserts were once trolls. Most of them are about specific rocks and crags. The first is the shortest, but it is quite characteristic: 'Near Hlíðarendi in Bárðardalur are some cliffs about which it is said that they are night-trolls, and that they were struck by the sun up there while they were looking for people to eat.' Another of these stories is strikingly like the verbal encounter described in the last chapter that turned Hrimgerd to stone. The premise, however, is more modern: every Christmas the person left behind at a certain farm while everyone else is at church is found dead. One year a brave girl volunteers to stay, and hears a voice from outside:

Your hand seems fair to me,
my keen one, but snarpa and dillido.

She replies:

> It has never washed filth,
> my devil, Kári, and korriro.

As the dialogue continues, the night-troll praises the girl's eyes and feet, and she responds that they have never seen evil or trod filth. Then the troll says that it's day in the east. Like Atli, the girl has the last word:

> Stand there and turn to stone,
> but harm no one,
> my devil, Kári, and korriro.

When people return from church they find a huge stone, which stands there still.

In more recent folklore of mainland Scandinavia, on the other hand, trolls are more likely to burst than to turn to stone. Indeed, in his general description of trolls in *Wärend och wirdarne*, Hyltén-Cavallius associates the aversion to the sun with an aversion to being seen:

> It is a known fact that trolls are seldom visible, except when it is cloudy and rainy. Then one can see them either in front of or behind oneself, but never as they go right by. Some even claim that trolls cannot bear to see the sun, for if they do, 'they burst'.

Later in his book, Hyltén-Cavallius makes the distinction between giants, whom the sun turns to stone, and trolls, whom the sun bursts. This distinction makes sense in that giants, in the recent mainland Scandinavian folklore, are beings who lived in the very beginning of time and who helped form the landscape. By this chronological reasoning, an anthropoid rock formation (and there are plenty of them in the North, some named after old trolls or giants) will naturally be a giant, since rocks and boulders and mountains have been around for a long, long time. It is also perhaps consistent that trolls should remain invisible even after the sun has killed them, as is the case with those who have burst.

If trolls can be large, small or the size of humans, and if there is little else about their appearance that marks them as trolls, what is the essential difference between trolls and humans? One main point is that usually humans cannot see them. This is captured in collective terms that refer to them as 'hidden people' (Norwegian *huldrefolk*, Icelandic *huldufólk*). One fairly common legend explains why. Here is an example from Sweden in which the narrator talks about 'the invisible race':

> Yes, you see, that's a race that we don't see. Eve had so many children that she was ashamed before God, and so she hid them. He walked and looked at them, there in Paradise. And then she hid the children, when he came, since she was ashamed that she had so many. And then God said to her that if she wanted to have them hidden, so it should be. And from that came the invisible race.

Sometimes Eve hides some of her children because she has not washed them. Sometimes the woman is not Eve, but Adam's 'first wife', Lilith or Lucia. Indeed, sometimes the woman is just some woman. However, more often than not she is Eve, and this is instructive, in that it puts the origin of the trolls in a religious context. Other legends about the origin of the supernatural beings tell that they were the angels cast out of heaven with Lucifer. These place the trolls explicitly outside the community of Christians, and this religious positioning is just as important as the normal invisibility of the trolls. As one Norwegian farmer put it, 'There is probably not such a big difference between them and us, because the same one has created them. But they are not Christians like we are.'

One legend type gives the hidden people a chance. It is a variation on the widespread story of someone achieving unexpected salvation, as when, for example, the pope's staff sprouts leaves in Wagner's opera, and the dying Tannhäuser is saved, presumably by Elisabeth's prayer, as the opera ends. In the legends, a human overhears the supernatural beings bemoaning their plight. Not infrequently a mound is open, and the human hears the mound-dwellers singing something like 'We are hoping'. The human dashes their hopes, sometimes with an impossible situation like that of the pope's staff. But the legends teach that God's grace extends widely. Someone wiser than the protagonist tells him he is wrong, or the miracle happens, and he goes back to tell the beings that they may still hope.

These legends are as ambivalent about the ultimate religious status of trolls as they are about their dealings with the human community (sometimes helpful, sometimes threatening). Thus to some degree, the trolls are like nature, or like life itself. As another seventeenth-century Swedish proverb put, 'There's seldom a litter without a troll.' (In Swedish, *sällan är kull utan troll*. The proverb relies on the rhyme between *kull* – used in relation to the birth of a litter of animals – and dialect *trull* 'troll'.) And 'trolls also inhabit holy houses' (*trollen bor också i heliga hus*). Trolls are everywhere, even if we cannot see them.

4

Fairy-tale Trolls and Trolls Illustrated

In the previous chapter I mentioned the story of the man whose bear chases off the trolls at Christmas, which as I said can hardly claim to be believable. In Norway this story has been especially associated with the Dovre mountains because of the version that Peter Christen Asbjørnsen published. Here is how he described the arrival of the trolls: 'All at once the trolls arrived. Some were big, and some were small; some had long tails, and some had no tails; some had long, long noses, and they ate and drank and tasted everything.' Just as the story plays with generic conventions, so Asbjørnsen plays with expectations about trolls. In a legend (believable), trolls might be large or small, and some might even have tails, but the long, long noses begin to err on the fantastic. Asbjørnsen was in fact the master of fantastic trolls.

Born in 1812, just before Norway was freed from the Danish crown and entered into a semi-autonomous relationship with Sweden, Peter Christen Asbjørnsen was a forester and, apparently, a skilled collector of folklore. In the 1840s he collaborated with Jørgen Moe, one year his junior, in collecting fairy tales in Norway.

Although we may have mental pictures of Norwegian trolls because of the striking illustrations by Norwegian artists, Asbjørnsen and Moe painted word pictures. The most famous of these is probably the one about the troll who threatened the billy goats who were on their way across a bridge in search of food in the high pasture on the other side: 'On the way there was a bridge over a waterfall that they had to cross, and under that bridge lived a big, ugly troll, with eyes like pewter plates, and a nose as a long as a rake handle.' Everybody knows this story. The smallest and middle of the three goats, each of which is named Bruse (a *bruse* is 'a hairy tuft on the forehead of an animal'), tells the troll to wait for the third, biggest brother. This the troll does, but when he repeats his threat – 'now I'm going to take you' – this goat has a ready answer. It is in verse, and in this translation I can manage only one of the rhymes:

> Come on! I have two spears
> with them I will poke out your eyes!
> I have two huge stones,
> with them I'll crush both marrow and bones.

Common descriptive words for trolls tend to be variations of 'big' and 'ugly', and here – like the clerical author of *Bergbúa þáttr* encountered in chapter Two – Asbjørnsen uses similes to express size ('eyes like pewter plates, and a nose as long as a rake handle'). Perhaps these outlandish similes helped to make this one of the best known of Asbjørnsen's tales. Such similes are part of his linguistic inventory for describing trolls: one, for example, is as big as three gateposts (*Rødrev og Askeladden*/Redfox and the Ashlad), and a troll princess has a nose three ells long (*Østanfor solen og vestanfor månen*/East of the Sun and West of the Moon).

On the whole, however, he doesn't use many of them, preferring usually just to call trolls 'big' – for example, 'a big heavy troll' (*Askeladden som kappåt med trollet*/The Ashlad Who Had an Eating Match with the Troll) – or to let the reader make that inference. The following is a typical way that Asbjørnsen conveys the enormous size of some trolls.

> At that moment they saw the trolls coming, and they were so big and thick that the heads on them were even with the tops of the pine trees. But they only had one eye all three together, and they took turns using it.

The idea of only one eye between the three of them, which they pass about and which of course the hero gets hold of, captures the idea of the strange bodies of fairy-tale trolls. Many readers will also recognize a parallel with the Graiai (Graeae) of Greek myth, who also number three and share an eye (as well as a tooth). Perseus manages to get hold of the eye and extracts from the Graiai what he needs to kill the gorgon Medusa. Like trolls, the Graiai are ageless or, more accurately, ancient, born thus according to some sources. Like trolls, they connect to nature, in this case water. And finally, like trolls, they threaten the world of humans.

Another enormous being with an externalized body part is *Risen som ikke hadde noe hjerte på seg* (The Giant Who Had No Heart). Here the 'troll' is of course a giant, and in the story the Ashlad (so called because he pokes in the fire and thus at first seems useless) rescues his brothers and their wives, whom the giant has turned to stone. When he and his helpful wolf companion arrive at the giant's castle, the wolf points it out and tells the Ashlad to go through the troll's door. What ensues shows clearly that giants too are trolls since, like the trolls in many stories ('Soria Moria Castle', for example), this one has a captive princess at hand, and he smells the Christian blood of the Ashlad. At the end of the story, the Ashlad has the giant's heart in his hands and the giant at his mercy. The Ashlad orders the giant to turn the six brothers and their brides back into human form:

> Yes, the troll was quite willing to do that. He changed the six brothers back into king's sons and their brides to king's daughters.
> 'Now squeeze the egg until it breaks', said the wolf. The Ashlad squeezed the egg into bits, and the giant burst.

The most common monstrous deformity of Asbjørnsen's trolls is extra heads, almost always in multiples of three (an exception is a seven-headed troll in the story *Mumle gåsegg*/Mumle Goose-egg). There are three-headed trolls, six-headed trolls, nine-headed trolls and even a troll with twelve heads. This creature appears in the story *Fugl Dam* (Bird Dam). Wolves and bears and lions guard him, and he is king of the trolls. He has kidnapped twelve princesses, but in stories like this these kidnappings are never permanent:

The prince signalled them that they should get out of the way, but they pointed to the troll and signalled to him that he should get out of there. But he kept gesturing to them that they should run away, and then they understood that he intended to rescue them and ran away as unobtrusively as they could, and the king's son hacked the troll's heads off just as quickly, so that in the end the blood was flowing like a big brook.

Although these fairy-tale trolls are large and misshapen, in most of the stories Asbjørnsen first introduces them with sound. Here is what three young boys experience, in the tale *De tre guttene som traff trollene* (The Three Boys Who Met the Trolls), when they get lost in a forest late one autumn:

> Just after they had lain down, they heard something that snorted and sniffed loudly. The boys listened carefully, trying to tell if it was animals or forest trolls they heard. But then they heard even louder sniffing and something said, 'It smells like Christian blood here.'
>
> Then they heard something stepping so heavily that the earth shook under it, and they knew the trolls were abroad.

Note how heavily Asbjørnsen relies on sound: the boys first hear the trolls snorting and sniffing, then they hear the terrifying words that signal who is at hand, and finally they hear the earth itself shake as these heavy beasts tread the ground. The smell of Christian blood is something on which fairy-tale trolls often remark. The religious ambivalence of the legend tradition has no place in the black and white world of the fairy tale. Humans are Christian; trolls are not.

Asbjørnsen seems to have found it effective to combine the snorting and snuffling of trolls with the din they make crashing through the landscape. Here is the arrival of the troll who is as big as three gateposts, in *Rødrev og Askeladden*:

> Just then the troll came panting along. He was so heavy on his feet that it creaked and crashed in the forest an entire

fjerding [a quarter of a Norwegian mile; *c.* 2.5 km] before him.

'Creaked' may not sound particularly frightening, but it helps Asbjørnsen use a rhyming pair, in the verbs *knake* and *brake*. This troll predictably smells the hero's Christian blood and threatens to eat him. The two play blind man's buff, and the blindfolded troll stirs up the forest and makes a racket as he stumbles about, before he falls into a bottomless lake and has to give up the princess.

Trolls in fairy tales are noisy indoors, too. In *De tre kongsdøtre i berget det blå* (The Three Princesses in the Blue Mountain) one three-headed troll makes his entrance this way: 'At just that moment the troll came rushing in and the castle shook.' After a while there is a terrible rumbling and crashing, and a six-headed troll arrives. Or a six-headed troll arrives like this: 'Not long after it started to boom and crash terribly.' Nine-headed trolls are noisy too. In the same story: 'Just then there came crashing and shaking, as if the walls and roof were going to fall in.'

Sea trolls make noise in the water, as in the tale *Fiskesønnene* (The Fisherman's Sons): 'Then it started to rush and roar [a rhyming pair, *suse og bruse*] in the water, and then a big troll came up.'

It probably goes without saying that trolls are ugly. The third troll in the story *Kari Trestakk* (Kari Wooodstack) is explicitly so: 'Just then along came the troll with nine heads, and it was so ugly that she could hardly bear to look at it.' It is soon uglier. Kari's benefactor and protector is an ox, and it fights with the troll. Before long the ox has poked out the troll's eyes and penetrated his torso so that the guts are coming out. Interestingly for the semantics of the word 'troll', later in the story Kari (a princess) is serving at a castle. She looks like the lowest and most miserable serving girl, except when the ox, now transformed into a man she can summon for help, endows her with beautiful clothing to wear instead of her usual woodstack (this is a fairy tale, after all). At one point, wearing her woodstack, she is to deliver the beautiful glove she left behind in church. When the prince sees her, he snarls: 'Get out of her, you ugly troll. Do you think I want a glove that you've touched with your filthy fingers?' Later of course, in a Cinderella ending, he realizes that she is the well-dressed beauty he has admired in church, and they marry.

As would be consistent with their large size and the noise they make, fairy-tale trolls are prone to fits of anger: in *Gullfuglen* (The Golden Bird) one was 'so angry that it was giving off sparks'. They are also not very bright. I have already mentioned the troll who played blind man's buff. He fell into the bottomless pond when the Ashlad went over to the other side and told the troll to come and seize him. Perhaps the most famously stupid troll in Norwegian folk tales is the one who has an eating contest with the Ashlad. Ashlad shovels most of his food into a sack he has attached to his belly, and at one point ostentatiously cuts it open, then goes on eating. When the troll falls behind in the contest, Ashlad suggests that the troll cut open his stomach, too. '"Won't it hurt terribly?" asked the troll. "Nothing much to speak of", responded the lad. And so the troll did what the boy said, and you can be sure that he gave up his life.' Fairy-tale trolls of course have to be stupid, for their narrative job is to be outwitted by the clever hero. For this reason, folklore scholars have classified tales such as the one just mentioned as 'tales of the stupid ogre'. The fairy-tale troll is nothing if not a stupid ogre. His dim-witted acts include believing that a boy who has squeezed whey out of cheese has squeezed water out of a stone; believing that the hero's gun is a tobacco pipe ('that's strong tobacco!' the troll says, after being shot in the mouth); believing that being castrated can make him strong; believing that hot lead poured into his eye can improve his vision, and so forth. He loses every kind of contest: in a throwing contest the troll throws the stone and the clever hero a bird; in a another throwing contest, this time with clubs, the troll believes the hero's claim that the top of a cloud is the club he has already thrown. Before starting a shrieking contest, the hero binds the troll's head to keep it intact while he shrieks and requests the same for himself afterwards. The frightened troll calls off the contest.

When these trolls do not engage directly with clever heroes, as in the various contests just described, their job is to disrupt everyday life – and in fairy tales, everyday life involves kings and castles. Here we learn of a king whose youngest daughter has gone missing:

Well, it would have been pretty bad there, even if he hadn't lost her, for there was a troll who made a constant mess and uproar, so that people could hardly get to the palace. Sometimes he would let out all the horses, so that they would trample down the field and meadow and eat up the grain; sometimes he would tear the heads off the king's ducks and geese; on some occasions he killed the cows in the barn, and he drove the sheep and goats over the roof beam; and whenever people were going to fish in the pond, it had all been driven up on land.

Of course it is this troll who has taken the king's youngest daughter, and he gets the eldest too, before Askeladden recovers them both by tricking the troll into the pond in that game of blind man's buff. Before that he had put an end to the disruption with the king's animals by following the advice of an old woman he had treated kindly.

This king's palace certainly sounds like a relatively prosperous Norwegian farm, and that is one of the charming characteristics of these tales. It also helped even these exaggerated trolls to fit into the narrative, since of course in the more believable legend tradition trolls lurked near farms.

Although these word pictures dominated notions of trolls for many years, artists had pictured them from as early as 1850. For Christmas of that year Asbjørnsen published a volume of fairy tales, styling them 'folk and children's tales' in the subtitle; the main title was 'the Christmas tree' (*Juletræet*). Like other such volumes, it was illustrated, in this case by Johan Fredrik Eckersberg (1822–1870), a painter who straddled the divide between Romanticism and Realism and is best known as a realist painter of high mountain scenes in Norway. In 1850 he had just been appointed to the Norwegian Academy of Art, and it was natural that he should be acquainted with Asbjørnsen. Eckersberg's fairy-tale illustrations are little known today, executed as they are in a style that does not meet the usual expectations for the exotic. The first troll in the book stands as an illustration to the tale *Gullfuglen* (The Golden Bird). The hero has just lured the golden bird down from the troll's tree, but violated the

Johan Fredrik Eckersberg, the hero encounters the 'angry' troll, illustration from Peter Christen Asbjørnsen, 'The Golden Bird', in *The Christmas Tree for 1850* (1850).

instructions of his fox companion not to take even a single branch from the tree. The troll bursts forth, 'so angry that it was giving off sparks'. Eckersberg's illustration hardly suggests such anger; indeed, the troll, who has shoulder-length hair, hardly looks angry at all. To my eye, he has a kind of bemused smile on his strangely bearded face. Unlike the king's son, who is dressed in some sort of generic medieval outfit, the troll wears only shorts, and he is hardly larger than the king's son. This troll holds a club, although none is to be found in the text; and he holds it upside-down in a grip that would be impractical if he actually intended to strike the king's son or anyone else with it.

   This troll typifies Eckersberg's notion of what trolls looked like: hairy, strangely bearded, mostly undressed and often armed with a club. He tripled it in his image from towards the end of the tale, where the fox has dressed up as a parson and tells the trolls, who are pursuing the hero, that the hero passed by ages before. "'Ha, ha, ha, ha", they said, and held onto each other. "If we've slept for so long, we might as well turn back home and go to sleep", they said, and so they went back the same way.' Eckersberg's trolls hardly seem consumed with amusement (nor are they holding onto each other, as the text states). They are about twice the size of the fox, which would make them about the size of adult humans.

Eckersberg also drew the three trolls from the Hedal woods, who share one eye. It appears that the club-bearing troll has the eye at that moment although, strangely enough, he has it in the third eye socket common to each of the trolls, centred in the forehead and suggesting that the artist had a Cyclops in mind. These trolls are a bit pudgier than the others Eckersberg drew, and although they tower over the figure in the lower left, he is, after all, only a half-grown boy.

Decades later, these tales would find the illustrators whose work would forever be associated with them. These now iconic illustrations

Johan Fredrik Eckersberg, three trolls with a fox dressed as a parson, illustration from Asbjørnsen, 'The Golden Bird'.

first appeared in the 1879 edition of Asbjørnsen's *Select Norwegian Folktales and Fairy Tales: With Illustrations from Original Drawings* (although Asbjørnsen's name appears on the title page, some of the tales were from Moe: these are indicated in the table of contents to the second edition of 1896). The list of artists was not short: Peter Nikolai Arbo (1831–1892), known now especially for two imposing paintings of mythological subjects; Hans Gude (1825–1903); Vincent Stoltenberg Lerche (1837–1892); Eilif Pettersen (1852–1928), a student of Eckersberg; Gerhard August Schneider (1842–1873), whose illustrations were printed posthumously; Otto Sinding (1842–1909); Adolph Tidemand (1814–1876); and Erik Werenskiold (1855–1938), perhaps the leading painter, sketch artist and lithographer of his day. While Arbo and Gude were near-contemporaries of Asbjørnsen and Moe, the others were not. Indeed, by the time this illustrated edition appeared, Asbjørnsen had been devoting himself to forestry and zoology for decades, and Moe had taken holy orders in the 1850s and was already a bishop in the state Lutheran Church.

Johan Fredrik Eckersberg, the three trolls from Hedal Woods, illustration from 'The Boys who Met the Trolls in the Hedal Woods', in Asbjørnsen, *Select Norwegian Folktales and Fairy Tales* (1879).

Peter Nikolai Arbo, Johannes Blessom hitches a ride from the *jutul*, illustration from
'The *Jutul* and Johannes Blessom', in Asbjørnsen, *Select Norwegian Folktales* . . .

Obviously Norway had greatly changed in the decades since the
first publication of the materials with trolls, and indeed folklore in
general had become part of the cultural scene, not least in literature
and drama, as I will discuss in the next chapter. It is therefore hardly
surprising that a new generation of artists should take on the challenge
of illustrating the tales, and thus of showing readers what everything
looked like in them, including a few of the trolls. And so the *jutul* and
Johannes Blessom appear in an illustration by Arbo, flying on the *jutul's*
sled. The *jutul* is portrayed as about twice the size of Johannes, but
otherwise he looks like a normal man, bearded and wearing a coat with
prominent buttons. This fits with the notion of believable trolls. But
there are fantasy trolls as well. Sinding has a nice illustration of the
giant who has no heart; he is indeed gigantic, standing at a mountain
pass gesturing at human riders below. Most important for the notion
of the troll, however, is Sinding's illustration of the troll under the bridge
that must be crossed by the Billy Goats Gruff. Like Arbo's *jutul*, this
creature is essentially a very large man, with shaggy hair that joins with
his full beard and moustache to cover the face that the artist presents
in profile, and thick arms and hands. He is peering up from under the
bridge, surrounded by rocks and a fallen log, with which he blends
easily. He also appears to be underdressed, wearing only short sleeves.

Otto Sinding, a giant frightens riders in a high mountain pass, illustration from 'The Giant Who Had no Heart', in Asbjørnsen, *Select Norwegian Folktales* . . .

Otto Sinding, the iconic image of the troll under the bridge, peering up at
one of the Billy Goats, illustration from 'The Billy Goats Gruff', in Asbjørnsen,
Select Norwegian Folktales . . .

But if the troll under the bridge looks like an unkempt human, the volume had something entirely different to offer. This was one of Erik Werenskiold's three illustrations to *Småguttene som traff trollene på Hedalsskogen* (The Boys Who Met the Trolls in the Hedal Woods). The first of these illustrations sits atop the title of the story and it shows the two 'half-grown' sons as they set out and the third, which occupies an entire page, shows their return. These are realistic drawings, with the boys dressed as such lads would be and, in the final picture, a detailed image of the mother at the front of the cottage, with a younger sibling in the doorway. The middle image, however, is completely different. It portrays the same trolls, who share a single eye, whom Eckersberg had drawn in his somewhat simplistic style some three decades earlier. Werenskiold's trolls look a bit like the trees in the twisted forest, their roots visible on the ground. We see only one troll in full, grasping a tree with a tree-like hand as he looks myopically through the gleaming eye. In this particular stance, the tree might just as easily be his knee. He has a long nose and only two teeth. He appears to be misshapen, as though he is permanently hunched forward. Behind him stands another troll who is bending forward. We see his nose from above and it looks like a beak. His twisted hand looks a bit like short branches between the two trees in the middle ground of the image. Finally, the third

Erik Werenskiold, the boys set off for Hedal Woods, iIllustration from 'The Boys Who Met the Trolls in the Hedal Woods'.

Erik Werenskiold , the boys return from the Hedal Woods, illustration from
'The Boys Who Met the Trolls in the Hedal Woods'.

troll stands behind, looking up. Only his face is visible from below,
and again we see the long nose and the teeth. The entire image is
dark, and we can imagine the dark autumn night on which the story
is set. The comparison with Eckersberg's illustration of the same
scene shows clearly how the notion of the appearance of trolls had
not yet been fixed. I think it is fair to say that from the publication
of the 1879 edition of the Asbjørnsen (and Moe) tales it was to all
intents and purposes fixed.

Another of Werenskiold's illustrations nicely captures the notions
of trolls as big and ugly. He illustrated the fairy tale *Følgesvennen*
(The Companion) with several striking drawings. Among them is
a troll who has a princess (temporarily) as his sweetheart. They sit
on a bench inside what appears to be a simple wooden cottage,
although according to the narrative it is inside the mountain. She is
wearing a light-coloured dress and dangling the scissors she has
tricked away from the boy, now her suitor, to give to the troll to
safeguard. Like the girl, the troll is smiling, but he has large, misshapen
features and only a few teeth. He has about twice the girth of the
princess, and his hands are at least as large as her head. But unlike

Erik Werenskiold, a happy troll and his princess sweetheart, illustration from
'The Companion', in *Werenskiold: Complete Drawings and Studies for Norwegian
Fairy Tales*.

Erik Werenskiold, the three trolls who share one eye between them, illustration from 'The Boys who Met the Trolls in the Hedal Woods'.

the princess, the troll is drawn with dark hatching and seems to blend into the background, which I take to be vertical planking.

The blending of the Hedal trolls' hands with the trees, and this troll's body with the planks, are manifestations of an illustration style that was to dominate: the blending of trolls with the materiality of the landscape.

Werenskiold was brought into the project by Otto Sinding, and he realized that he had seen very little of Norway. The now mostly forgotten marine artist Reinholdt Boll advised Werenskiold to go to Våga. He travelled through Hedal and came down into Våga where, like tourists today, he saw the *jutulport*, the entrance to the mountain used by the giant who gave Johannes Blessom a lift. Werenskiold made a few drawings and sketches there, but mostly, he reported, he looked. Years later, in the preface to a collection of his folklore illustrations published in 1910, he talked about what amounts to the artistic strategy behind his illustrations, especially perhaps of trolls:

> From the beginning I didn't think a bit about the concept of the fairy tale; it was so self-evident to me that I could not imagine any other concept. I knew only this: that I wished

Theodor Kittelsen, *The Sea Troll*, illustration from *Trolldom* (1892).

to have no break between the world of fantasy and reality. And such a break does not exist in the fairy tale. Troll and *nisse* and *hulder* exist there, such as surely as do we and everything that goes with us. And the two worlds are easily combined. One is the expansion of the other. It has only taken on new fantastic dimensions, burst the boundaries of the everyday. It changes, forms again, sits like a dream beyond all obstacles.

The artist who was to dominate the visual conception of trolls and other supernatural nature beings was Theodor Severin Kittelsen (1857–1914). Like many Norwegian artists (including Werenskiold and Eilif Pettersen, and also Henrik Ibsen), Kittelsen studied in Munich in the late 1870s, but in 1879 he was back in Norway. His 1881 painting *Vasstrollet* (*The Sea Troll*) took Werenskiold's conception of imaging supernatural beings to an even more imaginative level, and from the early 1880s onwards he was on the team that was illustrating Asbjørnsen's and Moe's fairy tales and Asbjørnsen's legends.

Vasstrollet shows the troll emerging from the sea, dripping with water and seaweed and apparently wearing no clothing other than the seaweed. He grasps his thigh with one hand, as if steadying himself. His nose appears rather large, with pronounced nostrils, and it seems to turn a bit to one side. The eyes are wide-set and bear a somewhat startled expression. Tufts of hair spring strangely from his head and face. But the most striking feature is the oversize mouth, gaping with a fearsome array of teeth. One senses that this troll is a part of the sea, emerging only temporarily for some terrible purpose.

Kittelsen was to do for land trolls what he did for sea trolls. Much of this work was in illustrations to the tales, but *Skogtrollet* (The Forest Troll; 1906) is the most striking example. Used as the frontispiece of a new edition of Asbjørnsen's *Udvalgte eventyr* (Popular Tales from the Norse), this illustration features a troll among the trees and mountains who might himself be a tree or mountain, except for the one gleaming eye.

Being part of the environment is in general what typifies the trolls of Kittelsen. One iconic image is that of the Ashlad squeezing

Theodor Kittelsen, the forest troll's gleaming eye, illustration from 'The Forest Troll', in Asbjørnsen, *Popular Tales from the Norse* (2012).

Theodor Kittelsen, a huge forest troll looks on in wonder as the plucky Ashlad squeezes water from a stone, illustration from 'The Ashlad who had an eating contest with the Troll'.

Theodor Kittelsen, 'The Great Troll on Karl Johan Street', 1892, illustration
from *Folk og trold* (*People and Trolls*; 1911), which depicts a huge troll wandering
down Oslo's main street, terrifying everyone except the playwright Henrik Ibsen,
shown in the lower right-hand corner.

Theodor Kittelsen, a troll deep in contemplation, *c.* 1900.

water out of the 'stone' (actually cheese) as the troll looks on. This troll has his left arm on a tree, and tree and arm seem almost to blend together. His legs, too, could be taken for trees. He has a long nose and dark mouth, and he seems to be covered with hair everywhere but on his hands; by contrast, the Ashlad's light sleeves and face stand out against the otherwise dark background. Kittelsen has hatched the lines of the troll just as he has hatched the forest, and the result is striking.

Surely Kittelsen's most amusing troll image is *Stortrollet på Karl Johan* (The Great Troll on Karl Johan Street) from 1892. Karl Johan is the main street in Oslo, running between the parliament building, which is visible with a flag flying on it in the background, and the castle. This troll is indeed enormous: he towers over the modest buildings of the capital city and has trees growing from his shoulder and neck. He is using an inverted uprooted tree as a walking stick. His shaggy coat and trousers are drawn with the same hatchings used for the trolls in the forests. The face, with its long nose, sunken eyes and missing teeth, could be any of Kittelsen's forest trolls, or the troll wondering how old it is, but there are observers who have discerned aspects of a self-portrait in it. If so, the drawing would capture the tension between Kittelsen and the Oslo elite, with whom he never quite got along. In any case, the joke is that Henrik Ibsen stands in the lower right corner of the image, unlike everyone else oblivious to the enormous being walking down the street and doubling the pose of the troll. Perhaps Ibsen is the great troll of the title?

Kittelsen was not a bad writer either. He composed text to accompany a number of his drawings and in 1892 published a little volume called *Troldskab* (Trolldom). It has seventeen vignettes, mostly named for a supernatural being of some sort, and in it Kittelsen shows the common idea of 'troll' as a collective term for supernatural beings in general. Each vignette contains a few pages of text and one or more illustrations. Many of the texts are like legends: more or less believable stories about named persons. Others are more direct descriptions of the supernatural being. A few have word paintings. These are interesting because they are, in effect, ekphrasis: Kittelsen creating text out of his own images. *På veien til gilde i trollslottet* (On the Way to a Party in the Troll Castle), for example, has an illustration

Theodor Kittelsen, 'On the Way to a Party in the Troll Castle', illustration from
Kittelsen, *Trolldom* (1892).

in which the troll castle gleams in the upper right of the image, while
from the bottom left to the top centre we see a procession of trolls.
They are shaggy, with long noses, and in typical Kittelsen fashion
they blend into the grassland they are crossing. Kittelsen's word
picture, like many of Asbjørnsen's and Moe's, invokes sound:

> Over the great dark ridges all around came the long trudging
> procession with strange shapes. Some were so old that moss
> and small bushes grew on them, others so ancient and crooked
> with age that they looked like twisted tree roots and had to be
> carried. There was creaking and groaning and rustling, panting
> and puffing, for they all wanted to be part of the group, to go
> in to the gold and glimmer, into Soria Moria Castle, which
> stood there and gleamed with light and shimmering tones.

'Soria Moria Castle' is the title of one of Asbjørnsen's and Moe's
most famous fairy tales. In it the hero, Halvor, rescues princesses by
killing three-, six- and nine-headed trolls. He marries the youngest
but loses her when he violates an interdiction to name her. He then

has to retrieve her from Soria Moria Castle, which is so far away that only the west wind knows where. After a long journey Halvor arrives there, just as his princess is about to marry someone else. They are reunited and, we presume, live happily ever after.

There is no mention of trolls going into the castle in this story; that is the conceit of Kittelsen's little narrative. It is also interesting that the drawing with the trolls approaching Soria Moria castle is in dialogue with an earlier Kittelsen painting (1900) showing Halvor on his way. In this well-known image, the castle is a glimmer on the horizon over a ridge, and Halvor stands, wanderer's staff in hand, and gazes upon it. The juxtaposition of these two images must have amused Kittelsen.

Another amusing ekphrasis occurs in Kittelsen's story in *Troldskab* of the sea-troll, the one with the gaping mouth with jagged teeth. This story is legend-like: a fisherman once apparently hooked a sea troll. Later he sees something strange on the beach. An otter?

> He poked it a bit with his foot. And then maybe there was life in it. It splashed and sprayed and snapped as if it were mad. Then Elias kicked it hard, and it rushed out to sea.

Theodor Kittelsen, Soria Moria Castle, the goal of Halvor's quest, gleaming in the distance, illustration from 'Soria Moria Castle'.

But before it got into the sea it grew and grew to a terrible ugly man who rose up to his full height and gaped with the gape of a sea-scorpion as big as an open coffin. And he bellowed: 'go ahead and kick me in the mouth one more time, Elias! But I'll tell you this . . .'

Elias flees, 'as if the devil himself were at his heels'.

On the whole, however, my impression is that Kittelsen liked his trolls. The collection begins with 'Skog-troll' ('forest troll') which tries to capture the fascination and fear of children hearing troll stories, and it ends with a sympathetic presentation of a troll who tires of his riches in the earth and allows the rays of the rising sun to strike and burst him.

The year 1907 marked the beginning of an annual series of fairy tales for children bearing the title *Bland tomtar och troll* (Among Brownies and Trolls). Obviously, the choice of beings in the title was to some extent – perhaps largely – driven by alliteration, but it still shows the transformation of the troll in fairy tales and children's literature. *Tomtar*, which I have rendered with 'brownies', tend in folk tradition to be workplace spirits, attached to farms, barns and stables, but also fishing boats, mines and even churches. The classic tomte is a small irascible old man who makes sure that the horses are fed and that work goes well in general. About the size of a small boy and dressed in old-fashioned clothing, he is seldom seen, and when he is, it is because work is not going as it should. Although I'm sure that it would be frightening to see one, the tomte is hardly as threatening as the beings such as trolls who populate the unsettled areas and pose serious threats to anyone who goes there. For children, meanwhile, they have morphed into friendlier beings, one of whom is the Christmas brownie (*jultomte*), who arrives on Christmas Eve, looks around for well-behaved children and confers gifts upon them. He is most effective with children not yet old enough to recognize their father when he is wearing a fake beard and pitching his voice below normal. Thus when coupled with *tomtar*, trolls are not likely to be scary. Nor were they in *Bland tomtar och troll*.

The annual featured newly written children's fairy tales by various Swedish authors, some of whom were quite notable. From the very first number, John Bauer (1882–1918; he perished in a boat which sank on Lake Vättern) provided illustrations for the tales. He continued this work in the series every year (except 1911) up to 1915, and those early years of the series are now surely better known for the illustrations than for the stories, charming as many of them are.

Although Bauer's illustrations are reminiscent of those of Arthur Rackham, his style is instantly recognizable. They tend to have a strongly vertical component, which in forest scenes emphasizes the trees and the light snaking down through them. His trolls are large and misshapen, but they do not blend into the forest the way Werenskiold's and Kittelsen's do. In *God kväll, farbror! Hälsade pojken* ('Good Evening Sir', said the boy in greeting), an illustration to Walter Stenström's *Äventyret* (The Adventure) from *Bland tomtar och troll* (1915), we have a scene that is to some degree parallel to Werenskiold's *Askeladden som kappåt med trollet* (The Ashland Who Had an Eating Match with the Troll): a boy and a troll in the woods. But here, the boy, who has entered the forest in search of an adventure, is giving the troll a friendly greeting. Although the troll dwarfs the boy – it looks as though the entire boy might fit in the troll's strange shoe – he looks as though he is scurrying away from the boy, perhaps in fright. Stenström's dialogue at this point is a bit different:

Then a troll came bumbling by with a sack on his back. It was the troll Big-Brother, the oldest of three brothers. He was ugly as sin, and the ugliest thing about him was his shaggy ears, which almost reached the earth, so long were they.

'Klufs, klufs, klafs, klufs', he puffed, as he went along.

The boy greeted him: 'Good evening, uncle.'

The troll stropped, wiggled his ears and bit and stared at the boy. 'What a dwarf', he said.

'I'm not a dwarf, I'm a boy.'

'What a boy', said the troll. 'What terribly small and ugly ears you have. Look at mine! These are real ears. I'm sure the princess will take me, just for the sake of my beautiful ears. You have terribly ugly ears!'

John Bauer, a boy politely greets a passing troll, illustration from Walter Stenström, 'The Adventure', in *Among Brownies and Trolls* (1915).

Without this dialogue, we might mistake the shaggy ears for tassels on a cap.

The dialogue is repeated twice more, with Medium-Size, who boasts about his long chin, and Little-Brother, whose pride is his long nose. Later in the story, the trolls' mother attempts to make the kidnapped princess choose one of her boys as a husband:

> 'Look at them', said the troll mother. 'Look at my sons! Handsomer trolls don't exist this side of the moon. Of course, they take after their mother. Look at them carefully, little princess!'

Bauer illustrated this scene. The three trolls stand side by side, and the prominent ears and nose are easy to see (Medium-Size seems to have his hand over his long chin). In a visual joke, Little-Brother

John Bauer, a princess shows no interest in the handsome trolls being shown off to her by their mother, illustration from Stenström, 'The Adventure'.

– 947 years old, according to his mother – is the biggest of the three. The princess is wholly detached from the scene and gazes into the distance somewhat above the viewer. Bauer's princesses are as striking as his trolls.

Where Norwegian lads regularly lop the heads off trolls, the boy in Stenström's story simply recites a formula, and the entire troll family is wafted away by the west wind. This formula is only effective when recited by a boy who is not afraid of trolls.

The story does not end here. It seems that the sister of the trolls' mother has become queen and is trying to pass off her daughter as the new princess. But when the boy returns with the real princess and tells people that the new queen and her daughters are trolls, people see them for what they really are. Both have long shaggy ears, long chins and long noses. They sputter with anger, but the boy calls up the west wind and away they go. With a word to his youthful audience and a wink to their parents, Stenström has the king say that the boy will get the princess and will inherit the kingdom: 'He is not afraid of trolls or of the dark; he likes fresh air; and he washes himself gladly. He will certainly be a good king.'

Medieval trolls did not break through into the modern consciousness. In the earliest translations of Old Norse texts, into Latin, trolls were giants, and this notion persisted into the eighteenth century: so, for example, Paul Henri Mallet, whose work on Danish prehistory, written in French, was also translated into English. When trolls went international, it was from folklore. As we have just seen, the Norwegian and Swedish popular conceptions of the fairy tale and its characters varied. The conceptions that were to gain international currency were those of Norway.

The mediator was Sir George Webbe Dasent (1817–1896). In 1840 he had a diplomatic post in Stockholm, and there took up Scandinavian studies, making his mark largely through translations. From 1853 he was a professor at King's College, London. Among his many translations was *Popular Tales from the Norse* (1859), which rendered some of the stories of Asbjørnsen and Moe. Among them were 'Boots Who Ate a Match with the Troll' (*Askeladden som kappåt*), 'The Three Princesses of Whiteland' (*Askeladden som stjal sølvendene til trollet*), 'Boots and the Troll', 'The Three Billy Goats Gruff' and 'The Twelve Wild Ducks' (*De tolv vildendene*), all of which have trolls as characters. In his Victorian translations, Dasent tended to capitalize those characters who were only described with nouns – the Wolf, the Queen – and so it was with the Troll. Readers had the word-portraits of the Norwegian texts before them, and so they met 'a great sturdy Troll' who warned: 'If you hew in this wood of mine … I'll kill you!' They met 'the great ugly troll' under the bridge, 'with eyes as large as saucers and a nose as long as a poker'. And they met other trolls, taken for granted as characters in the tales. So the troll under the bridge has been with us for more than 150 years.

The *Oxford English Dictionary* reports that the first use of the word troll in English (other than in Orkney and Shetland, where it was retained as *trow*) had occurred only eight years before *Popular Tales from the Norse* was published, in the strange 1851 'semi-autobiographical' novel of George Borrow, *Lovengro: The Scholar – The Gypsy – The Priest.*

At the beginning of the second of three volumes, the narrator has arrived in London and is visiting a publisher trying to place his work, 'Ancient Songs of Denmark, heroic and romantic, translated by myself; with notes philological, critical, and historical'. The publisher assures him that he has wasted his time, but the narrator insists on reading three stanzas to the publisher:

> Buckshank bold and Elfinstone
> And more than I can mention here,
> They caused to be built so stout a ship
> And unto Iceland they would steer.
> They launched a ship upon the main
> Which bellowed like a wrathful bear;
> Down to the bottom the vessel sank
> A laidly trold had laid it there.
> Down to the bottom sank young Roland
> And groped about a while;
> Until he found the path which led
> Unto the bower of Ellenlyle.

This recitation leads to an amusing discussion of literary taste in mid-nineteenth-century London, in which the publisher assures the narrator that both German and Herder have become 'drugs'. But even if this publisher has no use for the laidly (hideous) troll and the kinds of stories he in which he appears, Dasent was to show that there was an enormous public appetite for them. And in fact 1851 also marked the publication of the first volume of Benjamin Thorpe's three-volume *Northern Mythology, Comprising the Principal Popular Traditions and Superstitions of Scandinavia*. In 1852 came volume II, *Scandinavian Popular Traditions and Superstitions*, which recounted many legends with trolls and other supernatural beings. In fact, 'the wily troll' appears on the very first page of the introduction to this volume.

In 1863 Dasent published *Select Popular Tales from the Norse*. Aimed explicitly at children, this edition omitted tales that would offend juvenile (or parental) sensibility. It also was equipped with a few illustrations, one of them to 'The Three Billy Goats Gruff'. Signed 'JB', it certainly contains nothing that would upset a Victorian child. The third billy goat is butting the troll, who looks a bit like a sailor (he reminds me of the cartoon character Popeye). The entire scene is quite pastoral but utterly forgettable. I mention it here because it seems to me to suggest that the verbal art of the story it accompanies was particularly noteworthy. It was Asbjørnsen who adapted the oral traditional language for print. Such stories had been passed along in rural communities for generations, with both children and adults in the audience. Asbjørnsen retained or imitated the typical simplicity and directness of style and the repetitions that build so satisfyingly to the climax. This straightforward style was, in turn, easily rendered into English (and other languages). The Three Billy Goats Gruff was indeed a story with staying power.

Popular Tales from the Norse achieved success, so much so that Asbjørnsen and Moe made this unlikely claim in the Introduction to the 1866 edition of their tales: 'The English translation, by George Webb Dasent, is the best and happiest rendering of our Tales that has appeared, and it has in England been more successful, and become far more widely known, than the originals here at home.' It was thus natural that Dasent should follow up on this success, and in 1874 he issued *Tales from the Fjeld: A Second Series of Popular Tales from the Norse*. Both books have been reprinted numerous times, and some of the tales have been repackaged in other books. Together, these represent the bridge over which trolls walked from Norway to Britain and thence to the rest of the English-speaking world. There were, of course, also translations into other languages.

Of course, Hans Christian Andersen is far more known around the world than Asbjørnsen, Moe and Dasent combined. Andersen in fact had trolls in his very first published fairy tale, *Dødningen* (The Ghost; 1830), which was to be reworked and published in 1835 as *Rejsekammeraten* (The Companion). The basic plot is one we have seen in connection with an illustration by Werenskiold: the princess with the troll lover. In the earlier version the troll has black, tangled hair hanging in front of his misshapen violet-blue face, but in the second version, published in Andersen's 1835 fairy-tale collection, he has become simply an old troll with a crown on his ugly head. In the much later *Elverhøj* (The Elfin Mound) we meet the old Dovre troll whom Ibsen would later use in *Peer Gynt*. Andersen describes him not so much as a troll but rather as a king from the exotic North, wearing a crown of icicles and polished pinecones and clad in furs. Despite the presence of these trolls, I do not see Andersen as a major contributor to the concept of the troll since he wrote more than 100 fairy tales, nearly all of which are troll-free. In Danish a few have the *troll-* prefix, meaning 'magic', but once again the concept of the troll is hardly important.

Even if trolls had been important in Andersen's tales, however, they could not have had the influence that Asbjørnsen and Moe's did, for the simple reason that the early translators did not call them trolls. In Mrs Paull's 1867 translation of Andersen's fairy tales, which called itself the first complete English presentation of the tales, the troll in 'The Companion' has inexplicably become a 'magician', and the one in 'The Elfin Mound' a 'goblin'. But perhaps most striking is one of the few of Andersen's writings first published in English, 'Danish Popular Legends'. The venue was *The Riverside Magazine for Young People*, and the year was 1870: 'There is an old popular saying that Our Lord, when he expelled the fallen angels, let some of them drop down upon the hills, where they live still, and are called *bjergfolk* (mountain goblins) or *trolde* (imps).' Henceforth in this collection of well-known legends, there are only goblins and imps, no trolls. Thus the translator (identified as Horace Elisha Scudder) followed in Mrs Paull's footsteps. And so Hans Christian Andersen, far and away the most renowned author of the *Kunstmärchen* (literary fairy tale), and for many readers a mainstay of Scandinavian folklore, is not an important figure in the history of the troll.

Does this mean, then, that only the word 'troll' can identify a troll? The answer as I see it is yes and no. For me, goblins and imps are tiny creatures who lack the destabilizing force and seriously anti-social nature of a proper troll, so I think that in this case the words do matter. On the other hand, if 'troll' can function as a general term for supernatural beings, it follows that some trolls in some places are denoted by other terms. By this definition we could expand the notion of the troll far outside its normal domain. It is widely known, for example, that Japanese culture has a plethora of supernatural beings, and the *oni* certainly qualifies as a troll. Small or large, with a mix of humanoid and animal features, the *oni* often threatens humans but in tales is inevitably overcome by a hero. But besides this threatening function, the *oni* can be helpful or ambivalent. While scholars have argued that the *oni* derive from Buddhist Chinese origins, no one would argue a direct connection with the trolls of Scandinavia. What the *oni* and similar monsters can show us is the nearly universal human need for supernatural beings to represent what we humans are not.

5

Trolls in Literature

Although Dasent's translations could be adapted to make juvenile literature of Asbjørnsen's and Moe's tales, in Norway they were first and foremost mainstream adult reading. So influential were they, and so influential did they remain, that the novelist Sigurd Hoel proclaimed them the literary work that had the most meaning for the Norwegian people from the 1840s to the 1940s. It was therefore natural that some of their material should be replayed in other cultural areas. One important case involved the legends Asbjørnsen gathered into a frame story with the title *Høyfjeldsbilleder* (High-mountain Images), which takes several hunters up into the high country. The first part involves storytelling one night in a shieling. The second part, *Rendyrsjakt på Rondane* (The Reindeer Hunt at Rondane), has the hunters relaxing with no game in sight. They are exchanging hunting stories, one of which gives the title to the section: a wild ride taken by one Gullbrand Glesne on the back of a reindeer he had sat on when he thought he had killed it – over glaciers and near cliffs, finally across a river, before Gullbrand finally gets out his knife and kills it. Readers familiar with Henrik Ibsen's 1867 drama *Peer Gynt* will recognize this narrative from the opening of Act 1: Peer tells it about himself, but his mother corrects him with the information that it was Gullbrand Glesne who took the wild ride. And indeed Peer Gynt appears later in *Rendyrsjakt*, after the hunters have put up in a hut and are telling stories again. One of the hunters tells of a man who lived in the old days, Per Gynt (Peer is an older spelling of the name), who went up to a shieling one pitch-black night in late autumn and ran into something cold, slimy and huge. When challenged, it identified itself as the Bøyg (a rural Norwegian word for 'bend, bow, curve, turn'). Inside, it calls itself the big Bøyg:

> And wherever he touched, and wherever he tried to go, he felt the ring of the Bøyg. 'This is not a good place to be', thought Per Gynt, 'since the bøyg is both outside and inside, but I'll fix this contrary person.' He took his musket and went out and felt his way along until he found the skull.
> 'Who are you?' said Per.
> 'Oh, I'm the big Bøyg in Etnedal', said the huge troll.
> Then Per seized the opportunity and put three shots in its head.

In what follows, Per has continued dealings with trolls. One of them interests me, since it is in the believable legend form and put in the mouth of one of Asbjørnsen's framing narrators, but it sounds like a fairy-tale troll. Per is in a mountain hut.

> Just then a troll came and stuck through the window a nose so long that it reached into the chimney.
> 'Here's a snout for you,' it said.
> 'Here's some soup,' said Per Gynt, and he poured the entire pot of hot soup over the nose.
> The troll ran off and was carrying on, but in the mounds all around there was laughter and cries of 'Gyri Soup-snout, Gyri Soup-snout!'

Here Asbjørnsen makes Per the hero of a well-known legend type. Usually it is set in a mill, and a troll has stopped the mill-wheel from turning. The troll appears and says to the hero: 'Have you ever seen a mouth as big as this?', to which the hero replies: 'Have you ever tasted such hot soup?' Then he throws soup or, sometimes, boiling tar down the troll's gullet.

Our troll was named Gyri, and in his next adventure Per meets four other trolls, named Gust in Væren, Trond on Valfjell, Tjøstol Åbakka and Rolv Eldførpungje. Gust is standing guard while the other three 'court' – that is, by legend logic, attempt to seduce – three serving-girls in a shieling. Erik Werenskiold has a wonderful drawing of this scene, with the girls in gleaming white dresses and the trolls standing slyly behind them, blending into the darkness. In Asbjørnsen's legend, Per gets rid of the trolls and accompanies the girls back down the mountain to safety. His final adventure is as the protagonist of the legend we usually know as the 'bear trainer and the trolls', which we met above in the story of 'The Cat in Dovre'.

Act II of Ibsen's play is set in the mountains. In the third scene Per meets three shieling-girls who sing to trolls:

THREE SHIELING-GIRLS: Trond in Valfjell, Bård and Kåre!
Troll-pack! Do you want to sleep in our arms?

Here we find Trond in Valfell invoked on the stage. The other two names are required for the metre (troches here) and the end rhyme of *Kåre* and *vore* ('our' arms). However, Ibsen obviously inverts the usual narrative of the danger to lone serving-girls at the shieling. Instead of escorting them to safety from the trolls, as in Asbjørnsen's legend, Per plays the troll role, going into the shieling with them and presumably 'courting' them.

There follows the short scene with The Green-clad One, who is of course also a troll. Indeed, her reappearance in Act III with a child and beer lifts from a different Asbjørnsen legend, as does much else in the play.

Asbjørnsen's legend in which Per Gynt scares off the trolls with his bear is set at a farm at Dovre, the mountain in which Ibsen set the hall of the troll-king, also in Act II (Ibsen actually calls him *Dovre-gubben*, 'the old man of Dovre', in the original). Here Ibsen truly unleashes his imagination on the notion of the troll. His stage directions specify a large group of 'court-trolls, gnomes, and mound-dwellers' (*hoftrolde, tomtegubber og hougmænd*). The trolls wish to visit all sorts of violence on Per, but the troll-king muses on hard times.

OLD MAN OF DOVRE: Ice-water in his veins!
(motions his advisers to come closer)
Let's not boast. We've lost ground in the last years; we don't know if things will stand or fall, and one shouldn't reject

people's help. Furthermore, the lad has no defects and is strongly built, as far as I can see. It's true that he has only one head, but so does my daughter. Three-headed trolls are out of fashion; you hardly see two-headed ones any more, and those heads are only so-so.

After this amusing monologue, the king is ready to offer his daughter to Per. Per must agree to stay in the mountain, and he must answer one question.

OLD MAN OF DOVRE: What is the difference between trolls and humans?

Erik Werenskiold, trolls 'courting' girls at a mountain cabin, illustration from 'Per Gynt', in *Werenskiold: Complete Drawings and Studies for Norwegian Fairy Tales*.

PER GYNT: There is no difference, as far as I can tell. Big trolls want to cook me and small trolls want to claw me – same with us, if they only dared.

OLD MAN OF DOVRE: True enough; we agree on that and more. But morning is morning and evening is evening, so there's a difference in any case. Now you'll hear what it is: outside, under the shining vault of heaven, people say: 'Man, be yourself!' Inside here among trolls, it's 'Troll, be sufficient unto yourself.'

Thus Ibsen throws the concept of the troll back at the narcissistic hero. Literary histories report that the expression 'be sufficient unto yourself' was part of the political debate regarding free trade and import duties, and that early drafts of this scene played even more clearly with Norwegian self-satisfaction of the 1860s. The trolls are indeed isolationists, satisfied with their own world, even if not much is good about it. But clearly Ibsen also meant the supposed difference between humans and trolls to express issues of personal psychology and identity.

Although the play was published in 1867, it was not put on stage until 1876. It was a challenge for nineteenth-century stagecraft, and perhaps for that reason, although it was not unusual for the time, Ibsen commissioned Edvard Grieg to compose music for it. Probably the most famous piece is known in English as 'In the hall of the mountain king' ('I Dovregubbens hall'), and thus Grieg set trolls to music. (Interestingly, Grieg built a house near Bergen and called it 'Troldhaugen', or troll-mound. Many place names in and around Bergen begin with Troll-.) This short piece of music, or rather perhaps the theme that runs throughout the piece with slight variations, played by different instruments and in different keys, with a relatively heavy rhythmic intonation, is instantly and forcibly familiar, rather like the trolls it translates into the tonal realm. Grieg is said to have disliked it, and to have intended it ironically, but one can certainly imagine the tricks of trolls when hearing it.

Translations of *Per Gynt* into world languages waited until the 1890s: German 1891; English 1892; French 1896. By this time folklore had already brought trolls to the world, so readers and

Theodor Kittelsen, Per Gynt in the hall of the mountain king, illustration from 'Per Gynt' (1913).

audiences of the play presumably brought expectations to Act II. Indeed, in 1872 Edmund Gosse had reviewed the as yet unperformed and untranslated play, and he found no need to clarify the notion of the trolls:

> Per, outlawed for his treatment of Ingrid, whom he had immediately deserted, lives in the hollows of the mountains, and adversity makes for him strange companions. For he slips into an atmosphere of the supernatural, and holds intercourse with trolls and phantom-girls.

An illustration by Kittelsen of 1913 could also be a sketch for staging the scene in the hall of the old man of Dovre. There are shaggy Kittelsen trolls in the upper register, with their long noses and missing teeth, and the smaller gnomes and brownies in the lower. The small trolls who have threatened to cut and bite him gather around Per, who faces the old man of Dovre. The Green-clad One stands with her back to Per's back, facing in the same direction as her father. But the variety of expression of trolls on the stage is no smaller than the number of productions of this most produced Norwegian play. There is a Per Gynt festival every year in August, with productions of the play alongside Lake Gålå in Gudbrandsdal, that is, in the tract where the legends about Per Gynt were told. In 1906 it was performed in Giza, Egypt, in front of the very sphinx alluded to in the play.

Another possible connection with trolls may be found in Ibsen's play *The Masterbuilder* (1893). The connection of course may be with the master-builder story encountered in chapter Two: a troll whose name (identity) is revealed at the end of the story and who then in many versions plunges from the spire to his death, just as Solness falls from his tower at the end of the play (Act I also alludes to legends of a kidnapping, in Hilda's fantasy that Holness will carry her off 'like a trail'). In Act II of the play, when he and Hilde are conversing without Aline in the room and Solness is beginning to bare his soul to Hilde, she asks him whether there might not be a bit of troll in him:

SOLNESS: Why troll?
HILDE: Well, what do you want to call something like that?
SOLNESS: Well well, perhaps. [*agitated*] But I don't want to become a troll, the way everything steadily and constantly goes in me (*slig som det støt og stadig går i mig alting*).

When this play was first performed in Norway, theatre-goers surely knew their trolls, and when Solness plunges from the tower (the tower that had already been mentioned in Act II), if they bore these lines in mind they might well have thought of the troll who built all those churches. And we must not forget that Solness built a church in Hilde's village, with a prominent tower.

These were not the first trolls in Nordic drama. The little-known Danish play by Birgitte Catharine Boye, *Gorm den gamle* ('Gorm the Old', 1781), centres on the marriage of the daughter of Gorm the Old, traditionally reckoned the first king of Denmark (tenth century). She gives her hand to a Finnish giant, ugly as a troll, who has rescued her from Finnish ruffians. This troll turns out to be the Norwegian king, Erik Haraldsen, and in marrying him she augurs the 'marriage' of the two kingdoms of Denmark and Norway.

This sort of thing was to be swept away by Romanticism, whose first advocate in Denmark was 'the prince of poets' Adam Oehlenschlæger (1779–1850). His declaration of the new was in his *Digte 1803* (Poems 1803), which contains perhaps his most famous poem, 'Guldhornene' (The Golden Horns), a reminiscence on capturing Denmark's past. One of the other poems in this collection is 'Biergtrolden' (The Mountain Troll). Plot is of course not how we tend to think of Romantic poems, but here's the plot of this one: it's a mix of Norse mythology and 'mountain-taking' (troll kidnapping of a woman to marry). Using the god Thor's hammer, Harald rescues his Svanhild from the mountain. If we read it as Romantics might have done, the trolls might be stubborn adherents of classicism hiding away beauty, and Harald the poetic genius, or the genius of poetry.

In their own way, trolls were perfect for the national romantics, who sought to locate (we would say construct) a national past and thus a contemporary national image from the traditions out in the countryside, age-old and unsullied (or so they thought) by urbanization and burgeoning industrialization. When we think of national romantics, we think first not of poets (although there were many), but of philosophers like Herder and scholars like the Brothers Grimm, who in effect brought folklore to the world stage. If folklore was national heritage, then trolls were part of it in the Nordic countries, for trolls were recognizable local actors playing the roles of ogres and demons in the tales and traditions from elsewhere in Europe.

I began this book with an anecdote about an acquaintance of mine who saw a troll while waiting for a tram in Oslo. One thing I did not mention was that her Norwegian had improved to the point at which she could read fiction, and before she saw the troll, she had been reading a collection of stories by Jonas Lie (1833–1908) entitled *Trolls* (Norwegian *Trold* in the orthography of the time). It appeared in two volumes in 1891–2. By then Lie had won renown for a series of successful novels set in various social settings in Norway. A set of Kittelsen's drawings had been sent to his expatriate studio in Paris, with the expectation that he would write text for them, and although he never did so (Kittelsen wrote his own text, and *Troldskab* appeared in 1892, as we have seen), there can hardly be any doubt that Lie drew inspiration from them.

The trolls in Lie's stories are humans, or rather, there are trolls in humans. Lie states this explicitly in his introduction, which begins as follows:

That there is something of the troll in human beings, everyone knows who has an eye for such things. It is situated inside in the personality and binds it like the immoveable mountain, the fickle sea and violent weather – great and small monsters – from the individual powerful mountain troll and sea troll, which can deliberately involve itself in the stream of life, to the nix, the elf, the gnome or brownie, which plays havoc and places its whimsical fancies, tricks and capers into people.

Once when I was riding in a sled through a forest the horse shied at a large, frightening block of stone that lay and peered forth in the moonlight under a troll-like over-grown birch.

Since then I have met it again in an old lawyer – a strikingly wooden face, eyes like two dull opaque glass stones, a strangely certain power of judgement, not liable to be moved or led astray by impulses. His surroundings blew off him like weather and wind; his mind so absolutely certain, as if over centuries, that no one or nothing could dupe it. He was just an instrument gauge. Trolldom lives in that stage inside people as temperament, natural will, explosive force.

It is truly a step above and beyond that when it lives as anxiety, fear of the dark and hauntings. Anxiety is human-kind's first labour in the sentiment of separating oneself and lifting oneself out of the elementary, and along with it come all sorts of arts and charms to force it down below oneself.

And, to show how far this troll-stage accompanies the human being into civilized life would be rather useful and instructive, perhaps also rather surprising. The anxiety of existence, the great unknown about us, which is the basis for all religious feeling, constantly changes form and name according to the varying degrees of education. It lives in the mystical experimentalist as a tipping table at a séance, the knock of a spirit, and so forth, and in learned people under high-sounding scholarly designations like the 'fourth dimension', which in our era has more or less become the storage box into which one places everything one cannot understand.

There is certainly something in our educational and culturally secure life that would burst like trolldom before a clear beam of sunlight.

In the context of literary history, this is one of the more powerful statements of the 'new romanticism' that followed the 'modern breakthrough' in the North. We owe the term 'modern breakthrough' to the Danish critic Georg Brandes, who first used it in the early 1870s. In effect, Brandes put modern literature in the context of radical liberalism, and the 'men of the modern breakthrough' (the title of a book of 1873 by Brandes) composed literature that could be used in social debate. Lie participated in that movement, but as the introduction to *Trold* shows, he was willing also to look into individual psychology, into the unexplainable. To put it another way: there was scant place for trolls in modernist literature, but they were still there in the Norwegian countryside and in the Norwegian imagination.

The stories in *Trold* are *Kunstmärchen*, fairy tales composed by authors, not collected from or paraphrases of tales of the rural countryside. They are generally stylistically simple; many begin with something like 'There was once a man named X'. They vary in length and tone, but there is something both mystical and elemental about all of them. I find it quite disquieting to re-read them, even though I can point to the legends and folk tales Lie has used. For example, in 'Isak and the Brønnøy Parson', Lie writes about a fisherman named Isak, the very name of a fisherman who made it out to a supernatural island in one of Asbjørnsen's legends. The plot here concerns the *draug*, the man lost at sea. Isak fishes up a boot and recognizes it as that of his brother, who recently went down with his boat, and the bulk of the story concerns the issue of whether the parson will bury the boot in hallowed ground. Ultimately he does, but not before Isak has lost an eye (rather like the trolls in the Hedal woods) and thus gained second sight. Lie is particularly good at making the reader feel the fear and anxiety that beset Isak as he comes in contact with the world of the dead and the world under the sea.

Trold was already in print when Ibsen's *Masterbuilder* premiered. Although Hilde professes to be no reader, her question to Solness about the troll in him certainly echoes Lie's notion of the troll in people.

Lie's collection actually followed by a year a similar collection by the prolific Danish author Holger Drachmann (1846–1908), another figure who had been associated with the modern breakthrough but who turned to more Romantic themes in the 1880s. The trolls in *Troldtøj: Folkesagn i nytidsliv* (Trollish People: Folk Legends in Contemporary Life; 1890–91) comprise a variety of un-canny fauna, household spirit, mermaid, the 'moor-woman' (ground mist), the nightmare, the elf-king and so forth; even a basilisk. Most of the stories begin with a few verses featuring the commonplaces of legend and folk belief, but the narratives themselves play out what mostly amount to a series of nightmarish anecdotes that draw on those commonplaces in odd and interesting ways. Like Lie, Drachmann uses the troll as a conceptual vessel of otherness, of the uncanny, and moving from the trolls of nature to the trolls all around us and in us.

Just a few years later, in 1895, the Norwegian poet Arne Garborg published his cycle *Haugtussa* (I can find no better translation for *tusse* than troll, so I will render the title thus: 'The Mound Troll'). This work has gained international currency through the lovely musical settings by Grieg. The title refers to the heroine, Veslemøy (literally 'little maiden'), who early in the cycle gains second sight:

> Then she saw into mounds on the field, household spirits and water spirits, ghosts and trolls, and the drowned sailor with long hair.
>
> She went about constantly mumbling, with dark words, and sometimes she frightened her own mother; they said she had lost her mind.
>
> North in Lyngmark between three mounds is where she spent most of her time. And so she was called the mound-troll.

So, like the characters in Lie's *Trold*, there is something powerful and foreboding in Veslemøy herself. A subsequent group of poems in the cycle is called 'They want to take her': 'they' being a dead suitor. In the section entitled 'On Skare-Kula', trolls proper get their moment in the sun (metaphorically so: as we have seen, the sun has been known to burst trolls). Like Lie, Garborg deliberately blurs the distinction between human and troll. The easy distinction between good and evil is no longer possible as the nineteenth century draws to a close. Trolls can still threaten us from the outside, but they can lurk inside, too.

One of the most renowned poets of the later nineteenth century in Sweden was Gustav Fröding (1860–1911). In Sweden, trolls had played far less into the Romantic imagination, and perhaps for that reason they could be treated in less complicated ways than in Norway. Fröding's poem 'Bergslagstroll' (Bergslag Trolls; 1894) is set in the loosely defined district of Bergslagen, which is famous for mining. The narrator tells of an encounter with trolls who definitely fit into such an environment, as this stanza shows.

'There was clumping and clanging like the clattering of
scrap-iron,
and some had arms like tilt hammers,
and some had fists like boulders cast by giants,
and some had gaping mouths like the entrance to a mine,
and some had the roof of a coal-house for a hood,
and some glowed fire like a bunch of sparks,
and some had a snout like a crane for lifting iron,
and it was truly terrible', he said.

When they come upon the narrator these trolls, despite already having had a dinner of iron nails and spikes, plan to eat him. However, as he reminds them, the sun is rising. There is a terrible din, but the narrator is saved. 'And the trolls are just as terrified of the sun as I am of exaggerating and lying', he ends the poem. Despite the threat they pose to the human narrator, the trolls are fundamentally part of the environment, but not so much the human environment, as with so many of the early trolls. These trolls personify the noisy, dirty, gritty workplace of the mine. Like the mine itself, they can take a man's life, but the sun, which can only shine outside the mine, confers safety.

Although 'Bergslagstroll' is well known, another poem is even more so. 'Ett gammalt bergtroll' (An Old Mountain Troll; 1896) may be one of Fröding's most-read poems. It is often anthologized, even in translation. The speaker is a troll. His language is simple, and he seems fully aware of his trollness. This translation by Charles Wharton Stork is abbreviated from the original and not literal, but it does capture the style and spirit of the poem:

> The evening draws on apace now,
> The night is dark and drear;
> I ought to up to my place now,
> but 'tis pleasanter far down here.
> Mid the peaks where the storm is yelling
> 'Tis lonely and empty and cold;
> But 'tis merry where people are dwelling,
> In the beautiful dale's green fold.
> And I think that when I was last here,
> A princess wondrously fair,
> Soft gold on her head, went past here,
> She'd make a sweet morsel, I swear.
> The rest fled, for none dared linger,
> But they turned when far off to cry,
> While each of them pointed a finger:
> 'What a great nasty troll! oh fie!'
> But the princess, friendly and mild-eyed,
> Gazed up at me, object of fright,
> Though I must look ugly and wild-eyed
> And all fair things from us take flight.
> Next time I will kiss her and hold her,
> Though ugly of mouth am I,
> And cradle and lull on my shoulder,
> Saying: 'Bye, little sweet-snout, bye.'
> And into a sack I'll get her,
> And take her home with me straight,
> And then at Yule I will eat her

served up on a fine gold plate.
But hum-a-hum, I am mighty dumb –
Who'd look at me then so kindly?
I'm a silly dullard, a-hum, a-hum –
To think the thing out so blindly.
Let the Christian child go in peace then;
As for us we're but trolls, are we,
She'd make such a savoury mess then,
It's hard to let her be.
But such things too easily move us,
When we're lonely and wicked and dumb;
Some teaching would surely improve us
Well, I'll go home to sleep, a-hum.

Despite his dim-witted reasoning about his relations with humans, calling ironically as it does on fairy tales about princesses and trolls, this troll is trapped as a troll, trapped in the troll places, trapped in his troll body. The typical threat to humans fades away here before the troll's resignation to his trollness. One feels sympathy rather than fear.

It was probably natural that Jeppe Aakjær, a Danish literary figure always associated with rural Jutland, should have had added to this turn-of-the-century verse about trolls. His contribution was the poem 'Bjærgmands-snak: Ved en markfest paa kaphøje, 12. Juli 1908' (The Hill Man's Chatter: At the Market Festival at Kaphøje, 12 July 1908). At around midnight a group of workers challenge the hill man to emerge. He does, outraged that they would disturb the sleep of an old troll. He complains about the endless digging around his mound. He ends:

Once they stuck a spike in my thigh;
in my wrath sparks flew from my hair:
my wife held me by my beard;
otherwise I'd have landed a scratch on them!

In fact, many mounds were knocked down in Denmark for the marl that they contained, and the troll is probably offering an oblique comment on this practice, which can hardly have enhanced the landscape.

Trolls carried on in Swedish. Selma Lagerlöf, winner of the Nobel Prize for Literature in 1909, published two volumes of stories under the title *Trolls and Humans* (*Troll och människor*, 1915–21). Most of the trolls themselves are found in the earlier stories in volume 1. The second story, for example, is called 'The Changeling' (*Bortytandet*). Probably the best known in the collection, it begins with a highly imaginative description of a troll child:

> There was once a troll woman who came walking through the forest with her child hanging in a birchbark carryall on her back. He was large and ugly, with hair like a brush, teeth sharp as awls and a claw on his little finger, but the troll woman thought, of course, that there could not be a more beautiful child.

He is, as the title indicates, to be a changeling, and so he ends up with a human family and their child with the trolls. The rest of the story highlights the maternal instincts of the human mother. When people tell her the standard ways to get rid of a changeling – beat it, mistreat it – she simply cannot, and she protects the troll child even as she longs desperately for her own. Her husband tries to get rid of it, and when the farm burns down he throws the troll child back inside. The mother rushes in and rescues it. This is too much for the man, who resolves to leave her:

> 'I cannot bear this any longer', he said. 'You know that I leave you unwillingly, but I cannot stand to live together with a troll. I am leaving and never coming back.'
> When the wife heard the words and saw how he turned and left, it was as if something wrenched and tore inside her. She wanted to hurry after him, but the troll child lay heavy on her knee. She felt that she lacked the strength to push it away from her and remained sitting there.

In the woods, the husband meets his own beautiful son. He was treated just as the human mother treated the troll child, and the trolls lost their power over him because of his mother's sacrifice.

In this story Lagerlöf plays on the idea of the parallel treatment that is the denouement of many of the changeling legends: the humans beat or otherwise mistreat the changeling, and the troll mother turns up for a re-exchange, saying: 'I treated your child better than you treated mine.'

In 'Old Shieling Legend' (in Swedish, *Gammal fäbodsägen*) Lagerlöf employs several features of troll legends. The very first is that the shieling is a place where young women are vulnerable, for trolls 'court' them there, as in the legends about Per Gynt. The girl at the shieling, Ragnhild, remembers Grandmother's story about how the trolls called to each other about their intention to cook her. But this girl faces a new threat: a man she takes for a robber enters the shieling while she is making cheese. Just like the man and mill troll, or Per Gynt, Ragnhild has an exchange with the robber. 'Have you ever seen sharper knife?' he leers at her. She grabs the pot of boiling whey and throws it in his face with the retort: 'Have you felt hotter whey?' He then begins calling on the other robbers, by name, just as the troll does in the legend where he is blinded by a plucky hero who calls himself Myself (when the other trolls ask who is responsible, the blind troll shouts 'Myself!'). Lagerlöf does not use this motif, but she does nod to folklore about trolls at the end of the story; when the villagers find the robber dead in the shieling in spring, Ragnhild goes mad, like many people who had contact with trolls.

The first volume of *Trolls and Humans* also includes Lagerlöf's Nobel speech from 10 December 1909. A speech is usually not a story, but Lagerlöf was Sweden's greatest storyteller. On the train to Stockholm for the occasion, she wrote, she feels gratitude to all her family and friends but misses her deceased father. In the dark of night the train goes silent, as trains sometimes do as they run on, and she muses about the train taking her to him. It does, and before sharing the great news with him, she says that she is in debt. Not monetary debt: she owes the authors she read as a child, and the storytellers she heard.

Think of all those poor and homeless knights who roamed around Värmland in your youth and played cards and sang ballads. I am in debt to them for crazy folktales and endless pranks and jokes. And think of all the old people who have sat in small grey cottages at the edge of the forest and told about the nix and trolls and women kidnapped into the mountains! They were the ones who taught me how poetry can be spread out over hard mountains and dark forests.

The list of people to thank goes on, and when he hears the great news, her father tells her there is no answer to the question of how she can thank these people, and that he is simply happy. So is Lagerlöf, as she ended her speech with a toast of thanks to the Swedish Academy. That was the only time, as far as I know, that there were trolls in the Swedish Academy.

But trolls feature in the work of one of the eighteen immortals who were elected to the Swedish Academy. I refer to the novelist Kerstin Ekman (b. 1933), who has left her chair in the Academy vacant since 1987 in protest at their failure to take a strong stand against the fatwa on Salman Rushdie. Her novels are set in northern Sweden, and her crime fiction in particular is widely read internationally. The troll to which I refer is the central character in her *Forest of Hours* (Swedish *Rövarna i Skuleskogen* – 'The Robbers in the Skule Forest'; 1988), an extremely rich and complex novel. The central character is the troll Skord, whom we follow from the Middle Ages, when he meets some children in the woods and begins to be socialized, able to pass for human, through centuries of history (he does not age the way we do), until after some 500 years, love grants him a soul and he can die. Here again we see a Nordic author turning to the archetype of the troll to lend another layer to the complexity and subtlety that characterizes this particular novel.

The winner of the Finlandia Prize for best novel in Finland in 2000 was Johanna Sinisalo's debut, *Ennen päivänlaskua ei voi* (Not Before Sunset). In the American market the translation bore the title *Troll: A Love Story*. The premise builds on an alternative universe, in which trolls were discovered and classified as a predator species during the twentieth century. A young man finds a baby troll one night and decides to keep it in his apartment, with devastating consequences. Like Ekman, Sinisalo recycles the concept of the troll. In an interview, Sinisalo stated that the impetus for her novel was

Still from the film *Trollhunter* (2010) showing an enormous troll looming over the Norwegian landscape.

an incident in her home town, Tampere: a bear wandered into town and panic ensued, even though European brown bears pose no threat to humans. Sinisalo rethought the incident with a being that could pose a threat, namely a predator troll.

The Norwegian film *Trolljegeren* (*Trollhunter*, 2010), written and directed by André Øvredal, leaves trolls out in nature but imports them into a modernist genre-bending piece of amusement. These are the big Norwegian trolls of Asbjørnsen and Moe, but now there is a government conspiracy to cover up their existence, and a government employee is the troll hunter of the title. He is charged with oversight of the hidden troll population and, if necessary, exterminating trolls when they come into contact with humans. Three film students badger this troll hunter into letting them film him, a request to which he accedes because he is a disgruntled government worker who hopes that televising the circumstances of his under-appreciated job will possibly improve things.

The first troll they meet is one whose blood the troll hunter must draw for a test. This joke sums up the film almost perfectly: the government has both a paternalistic attitude towards the creatures it controls and a paranoid desire to keep them invisible to the general public. This troll lives under a bridge (joke number two) and (joke number three) billy goats on the bridge lure the troll up. Visually, this and the other trolls of the film are the trolls of Werenskiold and

Kittelsen, shaggy and misshapen, and several of their iconic images are invoked as the film proceeds. There is also a passing reference to an eating contest with trolls, invoking the tale in which Askeladden deceives a stupid troll into cutting open his own stomach. The troll hunter scornfully denounces such fairy tales. These trolls are real, or as real as computer animation can make them. The film also gestures toward all those noises that Asbjørnsen had trolls make, especially in a scene set in a troll lair, where we also learn that true Christian belief – not exactly common in Norway these days – can have fatal consequences if there are trolls around.

Trolljegeren is great fun, a witty and well-crafted film that deserved the international attention it attracted. A few other films have used trolls for horror (*Troll*, 1996; *Troll 2*, 2000) and family entertainment (*A Troll in Central Park*, 1994). The musical comedian Bill Bailey called the film of his live performance *Bill Bailey: Part Troll* (2004). Trolls have some way to go before they catch up with zombies, but they are certainly a presence in film and media.

6

Trolls, Children, Marketing and Whimsy

Although folk tales and legends constitute adult entertainment in the communities in which they are told, a conception of their suitability for children seems to go back almost to the birth of fairy tales, at least in print: although Straparola's collection bears the title *Piacevoli notti* (Facetious Nights) and was banned by the Church in 1604, what is now usually known as the *Pentamerone* of the Neapolitan Giambattista Basile apparently originally bore this double-barrelled title: *Lo cunto de li cunti overo lo trattenemiento de peccerille* (The Tale of Tales or Entertainment for Little Ones), and one expert on Basile wrote this about fairy tales:

> The philologists of the nineteenth century made accurate investigation of this variety of story, and put forward an infinity of theories to account for its origin. But in previous centuries such stories were merely a source of amusement and pleasure to children who listened to them greedily, then, as now; learned folk disdained to consider them, and they were rarely handled even by artists.

Although some of the French purveyors of *contes de fées* intended some for young readers, such as Mme Leprince de Beaumont in the mid-eighteenth century, for the most part written fairy tales moved in aristocratic circles. However, Johan Gottfried Herder, the godfather of German Romanticism, called for the following (to be published in German, the language that joined the disparate splintered polities in which some form of the language was spoken): '[A] pure collection of children's tales in the right spirit for children's minds and hearts, with all the wealth of magical scenes, gifted as well with the innocence of youthful spirit.' The author and folklorist Ruth Bottigheimer adds that Herder thought such a collection might constitute 'a Christmas present for future generations of children'.

The Brothers Grimm followed up on this call when they named their now-famous fairy-tale collection of 1812–14 *Kinder- und Hausmärchen* (Tales for Children and the Household). While our modern eye may see little for children in many of the Grimm tales (although we may feel similarly about Heinrich Hofmann's dreadful *Struwwel-Peter* of 1845, which was explicitly intended for children), it is certainly true that children are the protagonists in many. Indeed, the fullest study of a European fairy-tale tradition, Bengt Holbek's consideration of the collections of Evald Tang Kristensen in Jutland, Denmark, postulates a structure that the Danish folklorist Bengt Holbek called the 'children's tale'; this is a tale that does not get to a marriage but instead returns the protagonist children to their parents' home. And as we have already seen, Asbjørnsen' and Moe marketed their tales for parents, with special editions intended for an audience of bourgeois Norwegian children. Dasent's translations went after an equivalent audience in Victorian Britain. Here it may also be worth pointing out that many, if not most, of Asbjørnsen's and Moe's tales with trolls pit the trolls against adolescent heroes. The boys who meet the trolls in the Hedal woods are half grown, and a very common hero in the troll tales is Askeladden, the 'Ashlad'. As mentioned above, he bears this name because instead of helping out around the farm, he pokes in the ashes; he is thus, technically at least, a kind of male Cinderella. But he also bears the name because he is a lad, not fully grown. What is most interesting about this is that he is always Askeladden, and thus adolescent, in the published stories, whereas in the actual recordings from oral tradition he is not uncommonly Askefisen, that is, the Ash-fart. It is doubtful that Asbjørnsen and Moe could have sold as many books with Ash-farts taking on trolls, and it is also true that an Ash-fart perhaps need not necessarily be adolescent. In this, the published versions may therefore have been adapted for children.

In his *Troldskab* of 1892, which I mentioned in chapter Four, Theodor Kittelsen begins with the forest troll. He adopts the narrative voice of children fascinated by trolls and the deep Norwegian woods in which they live but also writes, I think, from the point of view of the illustrator imagining children enjoying his books. He begins with praise of the forest. Then the forest grows dark:

> Over there a mountain peak springs up. Wonder and anxiety gather around it. It got eyes, started to move, wandered silently upright toward us! And we rejoiced in the dread, we loved it!
>
> It was the forest troll. In his single eye he brought forth for us all the unpleasantness and fear, all the gold and glitter that our childish soul desired.
>
> We wanted to be frightened, and we wanted to be defiant. Little as we were, we still wanted to tease him, hit him in the heel, steal his gold. But most of all we wanted the gleaming eye he had in his forehead. Who would have believed that the ugly forest troll has such an eye!
>
> In that eye flashed and glowed that which can clear up day in the middle of the dark night. What you previously passed by and didn't think of, lay so wondrously glowing in it . . .
>
> You deep, still forest, we love you as you are: strong and melancholy. You charming children's picture book: the squirrel gnawing on a nut; titmice up in the pine needle, the bruin who growls in the forest. And the forest troll! It comes tramping with its head over the treetops – boo!

As a scholar of Old English and Old Norse, J.R.R. Tolkien knew trolls and giants, and he exploited them in his fiction. In *The Hobbit; or, There and Back Again* (1937), Bilbo Baggins and the dwarves with whom he is travelling are captured by the three trolls Tom, Bert and Bill (William Huggins). They are large and rather comic creatures who speak with Cockney accents and who would be delighted to cook and eat their captives. In this they fail, however, since Gandalf keeps their argument over the menu going all night long by imitating the voice of one or the other just as it seems they have reached a decision. Finally the sun rises and turns them to stone. Here Tolkien is of course playing on those Old Norse poems in which a human interlocutor (or Thor, in the case of a dwarf) keeps a 'night troll' talking all night long, as well as with the fairy-tale conception of the dim-witted troll. After the trolls are immobile in their stone shapes, the travellers take gold and weapons from the troll cave.

In the *Lord of the Rings* trilogy, the tone has darkened considerably, and the numerous trolls are no longer comic. In Tolkien's immense imagined worlds, trolls have a history, and there are various species: hill trolls, cave trolls and so forth; even half-trolls, as in Old Norse. All are aligned with Sauron, the evil genius of the novels. He even created trolls immune to the sun, the Olog-hai; these are far more dangerous than other trolls (although of course a cave troll is unlikely to be hit by a sunbeam).

In darkening the conception of his fantasy world and the trolls within it (and, I would assume, the complexity of conceptions of trolls and other beings), Tolkien was reacting to the terrible events of the Second World War. A different sort of reaction to the same terrible truths is to be found in the Finnish author Yrjö Kokko's *Pessi ja Illusia* (Pessi and Illusia; 1944). In this extended fairy tale, the little troll Pessi and the elf Illusia fulfil their love in the war-torn forests and woodlands of Finland, as they and other forest dwellers observe the war. In the first chapter, Kokko explains the work as originating in a moment during the Continuation War (1941–4; Finland, supported by Germany, against the Soviet Union, fought in Finland and former Finnish territory).

He wrote that he was driving in a car one bitter cold day not long before Christmas, as darkness fell through the dreadful wasteland created by war. He had hoped to write a fairy tale for his children but had not been inspired. As his breath froze on the inside of the windscreen, he tried to rub it off:

> Once more I rubbed the windshield with the rag. Suddenly my hand stopped. I saw on the glass a little creature, the size of a finger, whose features became clearer and clearer. Why, it was a rosy-cheeked little girl, wearing a snow-white fur

coat. The girl smiled at me and pointed a finger at another creature, which was the same size, and which I hadn't even noticed. There, in flesh, smiling at me, was a woodland troll, the kind whose pictures I had seen in storybooks.

'His name is Pessi and I'm Illusia,' the girl whispered to me, with a friendly smile.

'Pessi and Illusia!' I hadn't heard of them before.

The girl started to tell me about herself and about Pessi, how they had lived and about their joys and sufferings. I heard the song of birds, the smell of flowers, the roaring of the storm.

I thought the tale Illusia told me was wonderful. It was made up of a collection of tiny crystals, which at first were translucent and then became more pronounced and glowed with different colours. The crystals joined together to form an entity, like ice, which slowly closed the hole I had rubbed there with the glycerine rag.

I couldn't see the road any more, so now its bends didn't reveal to me the actions of war. I only heard what Illusia told me. I no longer even felt the cold.

Pessi-peikko (Pessi the Troll) is the pessimistic member of the couple, and Illusia the optimist. Surely it is natural that the troll should be the pessimist. He is of course one of the small trolls of the eastern Nordic region. Although Kokko specifically intended Pessi and Illusia for children, he did what to some degree Kerstin Ekman was to do for adults with Skord in *Forest of Hours*.

The year 1945 saw the publication in Stockholm and Helsinki of a little illustrated book bearing the title *Små trollen och den stora översvämningen* (literally, Small Trolls and the Big Flood) by the artist Tove Jansson (1914–2001). As a member of the Swedish-speaking minority in Finland, she naturally wrote in Swedish, and you will see the word troll in the Swedish title. The 'small trolls' are actually a unique variety: Moomintrolls (in Swedish they are *mumintroll*; I assume that the English spelling is meant to capture the long vowel in the Swedish). Interestingly, despite the title there is only one figure specifically called troll in this book, the central figure, Moomintroll himself. The other Moomin is his mother, Moominmamma. As the series developed, Moominpappa also appeared, and a host of other creatures. The first Moomin book to appear in English was the third in the original Swedish. There called *Trollkarlens hatt* (The Magician's Hat; 1948), it bore the more family-friendly and geographically located title *Finn Family Moomintroll* in the English translation of 1951. The Moomins live a gentle, somewhat Bohemian life in Moomin Valley, where they have numerous adventures as they interact with the other strange creatures there.

If the Moomins really are trolls, they are surely the strangest-looking trolls ever. Though they walk upright, they look like tiny hippos, with rounded bodies, broad snouts, pointy ears and longish tails. The facial expressions are only developed in the later books. Jansson once said that she drew the first Moomintroll in the early 1930s, when she tried to draw the ugliest animal she could think of when her brother had trumped her in a philosophical discussion by quoting Kant. Ugly or cute, the Moomintrolls were a huge inter-national success. The books have been translated into numerous languages, and in Scandinavia both dramas and operas based upon them have been staged. The art museum in Tampere houses an extensive Moomin collection, and near Naantali in the Finnish archipelago, where Jansson spent her summers, is the theme park Moomin World. There one can see the Moomins' blue house, Mumminpappa's boat, Snufkin's Camp and other delights. A well-stocked shop offers items ranging from Moominmamma's strawberry jam to books and DVDs. Those who cannot travel to Finland can use the Internet to purchase toys, plates and coffee mugs, inexpensive jewellery, porcelain figures, even Christmas tree ornaments. Although any consideration of trolls must include Moomintroll, it seems that 'Moomin-' is far more important than '-troll'. Nevertheless, it is more than likely that the word troll signalled to readers that they would be leaving the world of the ordinary; Moomin, on the other hand, would signify nothing.

The trolls of Asbjørnsen and Moe were presented for children in *D'Aulaires' Trolls* (1972) by the popular and successful team of Ingri and Edgar Parin D'Aulaire (Ingri was Norwegian by birth).

They are famous as writers and illustrators, and this little book shows why. It treats trolls as the collective noun for the supernatural nature beings and manages to include both fairy-tale trolls and legend trolls. The beginning shows that they know the famous illustrations, not least those of Kittelsen.

> In the old days, when only narrow, twisting paths wound their way through the moss-grown mountains of Norway, few human beings ever set foot there. The mountains belonged to the trolls, who were as old and moss-grown as the mountains themselves.
>
> There were many kinds of trolls: mountain trolls, forest trolls, water trolls, trolls with one head, trolls with three heads, trolls with twelve heads.

These trolls are creatures of the night, for they will burst and turn to stone if struck by the sun. Humans out at night run the risk of being captured and eaten. This all sounds a bit alarming, but much that follows is humorous. For example, the D'Aulaires thought about the practical problems of having many heads.

> The more heads a troll had, the more trouble he had at mealtimes, for all his greedy mouths shouted, 'I am hungry. Feed me first. It's my turn!' since even a many-headed troll had only two hands, he would be a very tired troll before the meal was over.
>
> Then he would need a good long nap under his quilt made of squares of silver and squares of gold. Some of his heads had bad dreams, some had happy dreams, some did not dream at all.
>
> The more heads a troll had, the wilder and more fearsome he was. A troll with twelve heads was twelve times fiercer than a troll with one head. But a twelve-headed troll had one great weakness. When he grew angry, all his mouths roared right into his twenty-four ears, and that gave him twelve splitting headaches. Then it was hard for him to keep his wits together.

The D'Aulaires tell their own fairy tale, about a lad who rescues twelve princesses from a twelve-headed troll, whom he beheads (multiple times) with the troll's own sword after drinking a potion of strength. The twelves make it sound a lot like Asbjœrnsen's and Moe's 'Bird Dam', and the potion of strength conferring the ability to lift the troll's sword like 'Soria Moria Castle'. They tell a few shorter narratives too: one about a lumberjack who squeezes water from a 'stone' (actually a cheese) and frightens a troll into clearing the forest for him; another about three trolls who share a single eye that falls into the hands of a boy. In all these cases, it seems that the images of the Asbjørnsen and Moe tales were what primarily inspired the D'Aulaires, although of course they knew the texts as well.

The D'Aulaires were artists first, and their illustrations to their troll book constitute an independent contribution to the troll portfolio. They favour light-coloured hair (dense and tangled), long noses, scraggly teeth and large lumpy bodies, often with shaggy clothing. Despite all that, these trolls look friendly. Like the text, the illustrations are above all amusing, and sometimes there are obvious visual jokes. For example, the text does not tell the Billy Goats Gruff story or even allude to it: 'Some lived under bridges – big trolls under big bridges, small trolls under small bridges. Some lived at the bottom of the sea, and some in deep, dark pools where they frightened away the fish from the fishermen's flies.' Above this statement is a colour illustration with a troll frightening some fish in the bottom, and in the middle a large troll, dark haired but with a white moustache, staring up at a bridge. Two billy goats have crossed it, and the third stands on it, head down and hoof raised. The troll beneath it looks decidedly worried, almost as if he is half hiding behind the rock that holds up the bridge.

Four years later came the sequel: *The Terrible Troll-Bird*. This bird terrorizes a village but is done in by some children's horse. The celebration is interrupted by the threat of two additional trolls, but the children are able to outwit them and all ends well. This book stresses narrative over the charmingly descriptive nature of *D'Aulaires' Trolls*, but it confirmed that trolls could still sell. Interestingly, it is a reworking of their *Ola and Blakken* of 1933.

A troll plays a somewhat pivotal role, if obliquely, in one of the great popular successes of young adult fiction, J. K. Rowling's Harry

Potter series, in the first volume, *Harry Potter and the Philosopher's Stone* (1997). Rowling is still setting up her characters during their first term at Hogwarts, and although Ron and Harry are friends, they find themselves put off by Hermione. That changes on the evening of Halloween. Hermione has locked herself away to cry in the girls' bathroom, having overheard Ron call her a nightmare. At dinner a troll-alert is sounded, and as the first years are being led to safety Ron and Harry realize that Hermione will not have heard about the troll, and they rush off to warn her. Rowling gives us a troll that offends more than one of our senses:

> It was a horrible sight. Twelve feet tall, its skin was a dull granite grey, its great lumpy body like a boulder with its small head perched on top like a coconut. It had short legs, thick as tree trunks with flat, horny feet. The smell coming from it was incredible.

Harry and Ron end up doing combat with the troll to rescue Hermione. Rowling plays on the stupidity but strength and tenacity of the troll. Harry grabs it and jams his wand up its nose ('troll bogies'), but it is Ron who saves the day. Using the correct pronunciation of the spell that Hermione had triumphantly uttered in class, he makes the troll's club fly in the air, and it tumbles on the troll's head and knocks it out.

The boys have now rescued Hermione, and she endears herself to them by spinning a tale about how she had, in her pride, gone off to fight the troll herself, and that the boys had just wanted to get her to behave properly. From this moment, the three are inseparable. Rowling's fiction is not the fluff of pre-school illustrated books or bedtime stories, and her troll portrait takes us back to the anti-social, threatening, misshapen and foul trolls of Scandinavia.

Probably the most famous troll is the one under the bridge in *The Three Billy Goats Gruff*. To cite but one example of its popularity, the BBC website mentions no fewer than four versions, adapted in various ways: a 'storybook' version in which children turn the pages by clicking a mouse; a bedtime story version ('The Billy Goats Fluff'); and adaptations as episodes of 'Big Cook Little Cook' and 'Fairy

Tale'. In these as in just about all the other adaptations of this and other troll stories for children, the troll is familiar and cute, not unfamiliar and frightening. It may pose the threat 'Now I'll eat you up', but nobody takes it seriously, least of all, as far as I can tell, the children.

To cite a further example of the empty threat that trolls have become to children, the three Billy Goats Gruff live on, every year, on stages in pre- and infant schools. On the Internet one can locate numerous scripts. All have parts for three goats and the troll, and most also have one or more narrators. Some follow the Asbjørnsen tale and diction fairly closely, while others just use the idea of three goats crossing a bridge with a monster under it. I have also seen a script for staging this plot as a puppet show. And on the stage I have seen an 'opera' (more accurately perhaps a *Singspiel*), performed by an infant school, of the 'Three Nanny Goats Gruff': 'Nanny' to counter the usual idea that heroes must be masculine. In addition to three nanny goats, there were numerous trolls, some ancillary butterflies and bumblebees and two narrators. Each child had a speaking part, and the singing was in unison. The emphasis was not on the primal threat of something lurking beneath a bridge, cutting off access to food and treating transgressors of the bridge as food; rather, it was on the children speaking their parts and singing together. The trolls were no more threatening than the butterflies.

Oakland, California, adjacent to my home town of Berkeley, boasts among its many attractions Children's Fairyland, along the bucolic shores of Lake Merritt. Opened in 1950, five years before Disneyland, this child-themed park had costumed guides leading children through a fairy-tale landscape with child-sized 'storybook sets', among them, not surprisingly, the bridge, the troll and the billy goats. After more than 60 years, these are still there, along with animals, rides and a puppet theatre. In other words, these children's trolls are not just domesticated monsters, they are part of the landscape that children navigate. Maurice Sendak's *Where the Wild Things Are* (1963) might provoke a child's nightmare, but I do not see how the billy goat troll, in his current state, could provoke anything but slumber, precisely, indeed, as 'The Three Billy Goats Fluff' on the BBC was intended to do. There Mr Troll is merely cross because he is kept awake by the noise of the billy goats crossing the bridge under which he lives. Mrs Billy Goat knits fluff booties to dampen the noise of the hooves, and she knits fluff earmuffs for Mr Troll and a fluffy blanket. Mr Troll snuggles down for a nice sleep, as should the children watching the story. In his comfortable slumber, Mr Troll can stand in for all the children's trolls in today's media-market world.

Still, it seems that when many people think of trolls, they think of bridges. It is only a short step to go in the opposite direction. After the Loma Prieta earthquake in the San Francisco Bay Area in 1989, a portion of the Oakland–San Francisco Bay Bridge, badly damaged, needed extensive repair. According to the *Bay Citizen*, as the repairs neared completion, the crew asked Bill Roan, who was both an ironworker and an artist, to fashion something to commemorate the work. After some library research, he chose a troll. "'In *Billy Goats Gruff*, there was a troll that lived under the bridge, and he was really mean and nasty to everyone", Roan said, "but he took really good care of his bridge.'" The sculpture is some 35 cm (14 in.) high, and in the photos I have seen, it looks like a goat with webbed feet.

As progress was made on the new span, people worried that the troll would be demolished along with the old span.

'It never fails – if I go on a radio show or something, I'm talking about Chinese steel or whatever is the hot topic, and then someone will call up and say, "What's going to happen to the troll?"' said Bart Ney, the California Department of Transportation spokesman who handles publicity for the new bridge. He concluded: 'Its fate is undetermined.'

Other under-bridge trolls would seem to have less precarious positions. In Fremont, Washington, for example, a neighbourhood of Seattle that modestly bills itself as the Center of the Universe, a sculpture of a troll lives happily. It is under the Aurora Bridge, built in 1932. According to the official Fremont website, 'old-timers' had sighted trolls under the bridge from the beginning, but the current sculpture dates to a contest in 1989 conducted by the Fremont Arts Council, to make use of the space under the north end of the bridge.

Five finalist proposals were put to a vote by the community at the Fremont Fair, and the proposed troll won easily. While Seattle has a relatively large Nordic presence, and Fremont adjoins Ballard, which has a historical connection with the Scandinavian seafaring community, I imagine the vote would have been the same in almost any city in the English-speaking world, so close has the relationship between bridges and trolls become. Putting a troll into the Bay Bridge strikes me as a somewhat ironic act, and I have little doubt that the voters in Fremont, too, were motivated in part by the civic joke of putting the by now almost cuddly troll of the billy goats story in a gritty urban environment.

The massive sculpture under the bridge in Fremont portrays only the upper torso and head of the troll, with his shaggy beard and long shaggy hair. Given that the sculpture is around 5.5 m (18 ft) tall and is considerably broader across the shoulders, the troll himself would be very large indeed. His arms and hands with unusually long fingers stretch forward, and in the left hand he clutches not a billy goat but a Volkswagen Beetle, which he may be about to devour. There is only one eye (a hubcap?), the left one, and that feature, along with the torso view, makes me think of Kittelsen's forest troll.

The troll has become very popular in this quirky neighbourhood (it also boasts a statue of Lenin and a Cold War-era rocket attached to a building). The troll has been decorated at Halloween ('Troll-a-ween') and Christmas, and the 'Rolling Troll', a 'bicycle chassis turned racer' that competed in the Fremont Red Bull Soap Box Derby in 2007, is now on display at History House of Greater Seattle. At that institution, intended to celebrate Seattle's various neighbourhoods, an oral history project called 'Fremont: Timber to Troll', began in autumn 2012. As a stroll around the neighbourhood shows, the troll also appears in other fashions, some involved with marketing.

And then there is this piece of marketing, from the ever-witty website of Mandolin Brothers, a guitar shop in Staten Island, New York, for a certain used Gibson electric guitar:

A Les Paul Jr is a slab body guitar finished in a brown sunburst with a single P-90 single-coil pickup and two rotary knobs. Simple, yes, but it screams like a rock 'n' roll troll who has just been told that the fare on the Verrazano Narrows Bridge has increased to $13 round trip.

Here we have again the association of the bridge with the billy goats' troll, but this one conjures up some of the more primal notions of the troll: noisy and downright anti-social if angered. This image fits quite well in the marketing efforts of a quirky used guitar store, playing as it does with the notions of rock music as anti-social and destabilizing.

Online, one can also purchase all sorts of troll items, especially troll dolls, and it is hardly surprising that there are websites devoted exclusively to such sales. One site boasted in November 2012 of more than 53 years in the business, and it must have got there early, because it has what I would assume to be a coveted URL: www.trolls.com. According to information on the site, a Danish immigrant, Ken (Knud) Arensbak, first fashioned troll dolls as gifts for Christmas in 1959, using acorns, pine cones, nuts, seeds and materials to bind them together. People were intrigued, and the rest, as they say, is history. The scholar in me cannot resist noting that supernatural nature beings in Denmark are small, as are the trolls made by the Arensbak family studio, apparently up to 50 cm (20 in.) high.

The business has certainly evolved. There are Viking trolls, harvest trolls, Christmas trolls, birthday trolls, artist trolls, forest trolls, some available with lit eyes and, for those who prevaricate, a custom option.

But here we have the potential for duelling trolls! The website damworld.dk claims that the Danish woodcutter Thomas Dam also invented the troll doll in 1959, and that only the Dam troll, from the Troll Company in Gjøl, Denmark, is the original troll doll. This site appears to be largely informational; other than a link, in Danish, to shops in Denmark that sell the dolls, I could find no way to purchase a troll doll. It shows a variety of dolls made of wood and rubber, some themed for Christmas, others in the form of animals.

There also exist what I can best describe as fan sites devoted primarily to troll dolls. One such is trolldollsguide.com. It reports that Dam trolls were made in 8-cm (3-in.) and 18-cm (7-in.) sizes. Most were made of vinyl, and many are collectable. This site also

A small troll doll holding a Norwegian flag.

explains that Norfin trolls were made by the Dam Company and that Russ trolls ceased sales in a settlement with the Dam Company. Somehow, according to this website, the Dam Company left a loophole in its copyright and Wishniks emerged as cheap imitations.

Another popular fan website is 'The troll collector's corner' (www. trollshop.net/trolls). When I visited it in November 2012 I found such delights as photographs of individual troll collections; instructions on how to make a troll cave out of craft paper and wood; a 'trolloscope' which promises to find one's own guardian troll (unfortunately I was unable to utilize this function); and a series of articles and images of trolls: observations, poetry, music, art, photographs (I quite enjoyed the dancing trolls from Arizona), information on related supernatural beings – even a 'Master trollologist test' to ascertain one's knowledge of trolls, with questions that often struck me as challenging.

Troll dolls clearly belong with children's trolls, as the very word 'doll' suggests. Ken Arensbak's story about troll dolls originated with Christmas gifts, and if they are misshapen, or even monsters made from parts of the landscape, it is in what can only be described as a cute way. At the same time, they do seem to appeal to adults, and especially to collectors, as much as to children. If nothing else, troll dolls at least offer an antidote to Barbie and Ken, whose popularity with children is well known.

It was probably inevitable that the plural *trollz* would come along. This sad monument was achieved in 2005 with the animated American television programme of that name. Although the programme focuses on five girls with magic powers who live in Trollzopolis, the trolls who feature in it appear to me (based on the website) to be troll dolls. If they visit the site and join up, children can design their own trolls, choosing hairstyles and the like: that is, designing virtual troll dolls.

The Dam website reports that their dolls will be joining the other trolls in mass media: 'DreamWorks Animations has acquired the film rights to the Good Luck Troll toys from Dam things in Denmark, and plans to produce a feature film based on the popular figures.' The imdb website reports that the film is in production, with the working title *Trolls* and a tentative release date of 5 June 2015. According to the information on imbd, *Trolls* will offer 'an origins story for the beady-eyed, fuzzy-haired dolls'. Perhaps this will resolve the question of who invented them in 1959. Even if it does not, I doubt that it will be the last troll picture show.

Epilogue

E ven if collecting troll dolls is an adult pursuit (and even if 'anatomically correct' troll dolls, of which I once saw an example, are aimed at adults), the forthcoming film *Trolls* is as good a sign as any that trolls continue to be popular with children. As we have seen in the preceding chapters, there is something of a direct line from the nineteenth-century fairy-tale collections down to modern media when it comes to marketing trolls to children. These trolls are occasionally scary but mostly friendly and reassuring. And yet there is a parallel line, almost from the earliest conceptions to today's media, when it comes to the anti-social characteristic that was once at the heart of conceptions of trolls. Associated with the anti-social are many of the other attributes of early trolls – attributes that allow today's trolls to play similar roles to those of the old trolls centuries ago.

This line would begin with the slang term 'trolls' for the homeless. I have heard explanations to the effect that homeless people, like trolls, live under bridges. Perhaps that is so – indeed, homeless people are sometimes said to lurk near the Fremont troll under the bridge there. But the origin of this usage could just as well come from the unkempt appearance of people who sleep in the open, who cannot bathe and shave regularly, aided, perhaps, by ragged clothing. More generally, this usage surely reflects the conception of trolls as outside of society, sometimes, according to what one reads in the newspaper, deliberately so. Trolls who choose to be trolls, who choose to cut themselves off from normal human society, raise basic questions about what it means to live in society, and what society means. Trolls have always raised this question, and homeless 'trolls' still do so.

An encounter with a homeless person might, perhaps, like an encounter with a troll, be unpredictable, but it may also be fair to say that many more people have opinions about homeless people than have actually had anything other than very casual encounters with them. I would suspect that even those living in areas with no homeless people may have vague fears about encountering them, just as in rural Scandinavia centuries ago many more people knew about trolls than had actually seen them. Trolls live vividly in the human imagination, then and now.

Vernon posted this related gloss to Urbandictionary.com in February 2003:

> Troll: Medical term; The patient population that frequents emergency rooms and I.C.U. units. They are easy to spot – all are non-compliant and wait days after becomming [sic] ill to seak [sic] medical attention. The first thing they have to do after admission is eat and take a shit.
> '*There are three Trolls in the emergency room, the* E.M.S. *brought them all and they have no transportation to leave. They all need to eat and take a shit so I guess they will be admitted to* I.C.U.'

These 'medical' trolls are clearly homeless 'trolls', and like the trolls of old, when they come into places frequented by the general population, they inspire feelings of revulsion. The particular signs of trollness here are not visual but behavioural, but note that here the basic bodily functions come to the fore. In modern society, they are usually hidden away, like trolls in the forests and mountains, and meeting them generates decidedly mixed feelings.

The business world has its trolls too. Firms that make money primarily thought litigation, alleging violation of patents, can gain a reputation as 'patent trolls': 'In recent months, tech giants such as Microsoft, Intel, and Yahoo have vilified the trolls – tiny companies that don't make anything but simply hold a portfolio of patents.' Such firms are trolls because they look normal but behave in a dangerous and anti-social way, threatening companies that behave according to the normal rules. They are also fairly invisible most of the time but cannot be ignored. For the 'normal' firms, encounters with these trolls are distinctly unpleasant. Again we have a direct line back to the original concept of the troll – a concept that is instantly recognizable and still valuable in providing a cogent term for what is meant.

By far the largest troll-infested environments these days are the Internet and social media such as Twitter. On the net, trolls are those who disrupt discussion lists, classically by posting off-topic or *ad hominem* messages. The term goes back to the Usenet, which was established in 1980 and therefore preceded the World Wide Web by about a decade. Usenet was the first large-scale discussion platform, and the various groups naturally attracted a wide variety of participants, some of whom were, according to mythology, more interested in disruption than discussion. Many sources suggest that these Usenet trolls were so called because they were metaphorically using the fishing technique known as trolling: trailing bait slowly in the hope that something will bite. In the case of Usenet newsgroups, the bait was the off-target post, and a bite was a response to it. They should therefore rightly have been called trollers, not trolls, but the concept of the troll was simply too powerful and useful. The original Internet troll(er)s behaved in a way that anyone familiar with Scandinavian folklore would instantly recognize: they threatened to punish improper behaviour and thus upheld social norms, in this case the norms of a growing and quickly evolving medium. I am tempted to tie the arena in which the late twentieth-century electronic trolls operated with the rapidly changing late nineteenth- and early twentieth-century rural society of Scandinavia, which gave us the classical trolls of fairy tale, legend and folk belief. Perhaps the faster things change, the more the norms are enforced not by the community but by less-visible forces from outside it.

That was then, this is now. Urbandictionary.com has 35 pages of definitions of troll, and the vast majority aim at nuisances and pests on the Internet. A much smaller number talk about the characters in folklore and a few others seem to be inspired inventions. Since it turns up more than once, I am willing to imagine that *troll* can define a person from Michigan who lives in the lower portion of the state, that is, below the (Mackinaw) bridge, which separates lower Michigan from the Upper Peninsula. (According to these entries, the antonym to *troll* in this meaning is *Yooper*.) There are even a few glosses joining the folklore and Internet trolls by suggesting that the latter are ugly and live in caves. And many just suggest that trolls are losers.

In an article on computer/howstuffworks.com, Jonathan Strickland wrote, 'Just as it's common for people to call any kind of malware a computer virus, it's not unusual for people to call any kind of disruptive person online a troll.' According to Strickland, there are many kinds of Internet trolls alongside the original Usenet variety:

trolls who pose as 'newbies' (clueless new members of the discussion group) and pose naive questions hoping to start a fight among more experienced members

trolls who rely on insults, hoping to provoke angry responses

sneaky trolls, who pretend to be sincere but pose questions intended to shake discussants' beliefs about the topic

colluding trolls, who work together to disrupt a single discussion group

griefers: trolls who seek to disrupt online games

On Urbandictionary.com I have seen suggestions for other subcategories. The simplest involves a distinction between good trolls and bad trolls. This may sound simple, but in fact trolls have always been both good and bad: good in upholding norms and proper behaviour, bad in threatening people and sometimes carrying out those threats.

Far more complex was the set of categories suggested by a user called 'sndansoenrnarongb[enqa' in a message posted on 17 August 2011. I quote it because it echoes, to my ear, the complexity that has always characterized trolls. The details have changed; these trolls are not large or small, shaggy or misshapen, changers of shapes or perceptions, but they still blur categories, and they still disrupt:

plain trolls
bashing trolls
smartass trolls
non-caring trolls
opinion trolls
12-year old trolls
blaming trolls

Today the action is on Twitter, where trolls hide behind their anonymity to post crude and threatening tweets, much of it misogynous. The verb 'troll' still exists: one troll was outed by his victim, the Cambridge professor Mary Beard, who simply reposted his offensive message. In an article of 29 July 2013 entitled 'Mary Beard Silences Offensive Twitter Troll', *The Guardian* reported:

> Fellow users immediately condemned Rawlings [the troll] and within minutes he responded: 'I sincerely apologise for my trolling. I was wrong and very rude. Hope this can be forgotten and forgiven.'
> He later added: 'I feel this had been a good lesson for me. Thanks 4 showing me the error of my ways.'
> Beard offered to delete her retweet if the original message was deleted.
> She said exposing trolls was the best tactic.

It would seem that the original notion of electronic trolling, of casting something offbeat into an Internet pond to see who will bite, has increasingly moved towards the notion of the troll as deeply disruptive and antisocial. The original trolls in Scandinavia threatened to kill humans who came into contact with them, and so do these trolls, although they add threats of rape when their victim is female. When the Bank of England approved putting Jane Austen's picture on £10 notes, vicious tweets began to appear in the inbox of Caroline Criado-Perez, who had led the campaign for a woman's face on future currency. And as Katrin Bennhold reported in the *New York Times* on 4 August 2013 ('Bid to Honor Austen is not Universally Acknowledged'), several other prominent women also received death threats and others tweeted abuse, and in fact arrests were made. Bennhold went on: 'Scotland Yard's electronic-crime unit is investigating the Twitter attacks involving mostly anonymous Internet users, so-called trolls.' As Twitter looks for technological solutions, its users call for self-policing and restraint. But it does seem that the medium offers the potential for the ugly dark side of some users to emerge.

According to Jonathan Strickland, on the Internet there are discussion groups run by and for trolls, where they can discuss their disruptive activities or post vulgar messages or images. I visited the one he mentioned, and I indeed found vulgar messages and images, many of them pornographic. My research was not thorough, but in the brief moments I spent reviewing posts I saw no discussion of trolling. In any case, since all posts to this particular site are anonymous, all participants lurk in the shadows, as do Twitter trolls, and in that they surely do resemble the trolls of tradition.

In the old tradition, people who spent time in the world of the trolls described it mostly as unpleasant, and I cannot say that my brief visit to the world of today's trolls was in any way pleasant. Yet I experienced, ever more strongly, the fact that we cannot truly know trolls. If we could, they would not be trolls. This holds for the very first trolls, found in Viking Age poetry, through the trolls who populated the wilds of Scandinavia, to the trolls in books, films and the Internet. Trolls are what we are not, or what we think we are not. Or was Jonas Lie right? Could there be a bit of troll in each of us?

Sources and Further Reading

Works on Trolls in General

The most lively piece of writing on trolls is Martin Arnold's 'Hvat er troll nema þat? The Cultural History of the Troll', in Tom Shippey, ed., *The Shadow Walkers: Jacob Grimm's Mythology of the Monstrous* (Tempe, AZ, 2005), pp. 111–55. As the title suggests, it is aimed at a scholarly audience, but the main argument is set forth clearly. Arnold proposes a development from myth (when trolls were trolls), through a medieval narrative mode (when trolls shade into humans), to more recent folklore (when trolls are the monstrous Other often set up in opposition to things Christian). As Arnold puts it, 'There is, I have suggested, a general movement through myth, saga (early and late), and folktale, whereby the troll is initially dysfunctional, then dystopian, then most latterly an agency of ideological disquiet' (p. 155). We scholars often seek historical development, and Arnold has found one. In this book I have to a greater extent stressed the characteristics of trolls in the contexts in which we meet them, and I have given more attention to similarities than to differences that can be ranged in a historical context.

There are few book-length treatments of trolls. Elisabeth Hartmann's published dissertation, *Die Trollvorstellungen in den Sagen und Märchen der skandinavischen Völker* (Stuttgart and Berlin, 1936), nods to the older traditions and offers a survey of trolls in the legends and folk tales of more recent folklore. It is thorough but outdated. For the medieval material, there is Katja Schulz's *Riesen: von Wissenshutern und Wildnisbewohnern in Edda und Saga* (Heidelberg, 2004), a published dissertation that treats the Old Norse traditions (very thoroughly) and does so under the rubric of giants. In a shorter treatment, 'The Trollish Acts of Þorgrímr the Witch: The Meanings of Troll and Ergi in Medieval Iceland' in *Saga-Book*, XXXII (2008), pp. 39–68, Ármann Jakobsson finds that the word troll in high medieval Iceland could denote no fewer than fourteen categories:

>Icelandic fairy-tale trolls
>Humans who look like trolls
>Troll as a pejorative metaphor
>Evil spirits and ghosts
>Blámenn
>Animal monsters
>Pagan figures and opponents of Christianity
>Those who spoil wells (by urinating in them)
>Asocial behaviour
>Berserks
>As an expression of strength
>Foreigners

Camilla Asplund Ingemark, *The Genre of Trolls* (Åbo, 2004), surveys the concepts of the troll in Swedish-language archived material in Finland from the nineteenth and early twentieth centuries and shows how conceptions of the troll there can be related to religious doctrine (thus supporting the broad contours of Arnold's argument), as well as some nuanced and insightful readings of individual narratives. Beyond that, there are many works with titles like *Trolls*, some of which I have taken up above, but no other book-length surveys of which I am aware.

A helpful websites is trollmoon.com.

Introduction

The paradigm of the empirical encounter with the supernatural, leading to the production of what some folklorists have called a memorate (that is, a first-hand account of a supernatural experience), was set forth by Lauri Honko, 'Memorates and the Study of Folk Belief', *Journal of the Folklore Institute*, I/5–19 (1964), and builds on his earlier study of spirit belief in Ingria, *Geisterglaube in Ingermanland* (Helsinki, 1962).

The Grimms issued their famous statement distinguishing 'more poetic' folk tales from 'more historical' legends in the preface to their collection of German legends, *Deutsche Sagen* (1816–18).

Helgi the Lean and his wavering beliefs are found in *Landnámabók*, the Icelandic 'Books of Settlements', ed. Jakob Benediktsson (Reykjavik, 1968), p. 250.

The most radical postulation of a 'folk' was offered by Alan Dundes, who suggested that a folk group could be as few as two persons with at least one thing in common. It was first expressed in Dundes, *The Study of Folklore* (Englewood Cliffs, NJ, 1965) and restated in 1980: 'Who Are the Folk', in his *Interpreting Folklore* (Bloomington, IN, 1980).

On legends, see Linda Dégh, *Legend and Belief: Dialectics of a Folklore Genre* (Bloomington, IN, 2001); Timothy R. Tangherlini, 'It Happened Not Too Far From Here: A Survey of Legend Theory and Characterization', *Western Folklore*, XLI (1990), pp. 371–90; and Tangherlini, *Interpreting Legend: Danish Storytellers and their Repertories* (New York, 1994).

All the etymological handbooks have information on possible origins of the word(s) for troll. A recent discussion in English may be found in Arnold's article, discussed above.

At the end of the chapter I quote from two disparate Old Norse works: *Hjálmpes saga ok Ölvis* is one of the so-called *fornaldarsögur*, on which see chapter Two; *Málsháttkvæði* is a skaldic poem, on which see chapter One. The translations are my own, as is the case throughout the book unless otherwise indicated.

1 The Earliest Trolls

Skaldic poetry dates back to the Viking Age and continued through the Middle Ages, but the earliest material is recorded only in much later manuscripts. I quote from standard editions. Often I used Finnur Jónsson, *Den norsk-islandske skjaldedigtning* (1912–15), but when available I used the in-progress new edition being worked on by a team of scholars, including in this chapter Diana Whaley's edition of and commentary to Þjóðólfr Arnórsson's *Sexstefja* in *Poetry from the Kings' Sagas*, vol. II: *From c. 1035 to c. 1300*, ed. Kari Ellen Gade (Turnhout, 2009), pp. 177–281. Sometimes instead I used editions of works in which the verses were recorded, as with the verses exchanged between Bragi and the troll woman. For that I consulted the edition by Anthony Faulkes: *Snorri Sturluson: Edda*, which has separate volumes for the various parts: *Prologue: Gylfaginning*, 2nd edn (London, 2005); *Skáldskaparmál*, 2 vols (London, 1998); and *Háttatal*, 2nd edn (London, 2007). For the translations of Snorri's *Edda* I quoted the reliable translation by Faulkes, *Snorri Sturluson: Edda* (London, 1987), occasionally adapting it for clarity. Old Norse poetry is fascinating, if challenging; an engaging treatment is that of Margaret Clunies Ross, *A History of Old Norse Poetics* (Cambridge, 2005). The kenning system relies on knowledge of the mythology, on which I can recommend reading Snorri, the *Poetic Edda* (see below) and, for secondary treatments, my own *Handbook of Old Norse Mythology* (London, 2001). For poetry of the so-called 'Eddic' sort, including, for example, *Völuspá*, I consulted the standard edition by Gustav Neckel and Hans Kuhn, *Edda: die Lieder des Codex Regius nebst verwandten Denkmälern*, 5th edn (Heidelberg, 1983), and used the translation of Carolyne Larrington, *The Poetic Edda* (Oxford, 1996), sometimes adapting it for clarity. For Snorri's *Heimskringla*, I consulted and translated from the standard edition by Bjarni Aðalbjarnarson *Heimskringla*, 3 vols (Reykjavík, 1941–51). For other sagas, too, I consulted and translated from standard editions: *Kormáks saga*; *Grettis saga*; *Orms þáttr Stórólfssonar*. Many of these have appeared in the series *Íslenzk fornrit* (Bjarni Aðalbjarnarson's edition of *Heimskringla*, for example), and sometimes I just give the volume number in that series. *Landnámabók*, too, is edited in the fornrit series, by Jakob Benediktsson (Reykjavík, 1968).

2 Medieval Trolls

For *Bergbúa þáttr* (a *þáttr* is in this context an independent short narrative), I consulted the fornrit edition by Þórhallur Vilmundarson and Bjarni Vilhjálmsson (Reykjavík, 1991). The quotation is on p. 442. For notion of a connection with the Hallmundarhraun eruption,

I am indebted to an email exchange with the Icelandic geologist Árni Hjartarson, a specialist in hydrogeology and geothermal heat, who kindly sent me the abstract of a lecture he had given at the Icelandic Society for Natural Sciences on Hallmundarkviða and Hallmundarhraun. In his reasoning he was following up on a suggestion by Páll Bergþórsson, published in *Lesbók Morgunblaðsins*, 2006.

Illuga saga Gríðarfóstra is one of the so-called *fornaldarsögur* ('sagas of the ancient age'), sometimes known in English as mythic–heroic or legendary sagas. The 'ancient age' means 'prehistoric' times, in the Icelandic sense – that is, before Iceland was settled in the early Viking Age. These sagas tend towards the fantastic. For this book, I consulted most of them in the convenient edition of Guðni Jónsson, *Fornaldarsögur Norðrlanda*, 4 vols (Hafnarfjörður, 1959), and I sometimes choose to refer to them, together with such translated materials as *Karlamagnús saga*, as romances. (I consulted the edition by Agnete Loth, Copenhagen, 1980). The exceptions to my use of the Guðni Jónsson edition are the saga of Arrow-Odd: *Örvar-Odds saga*, ed. R. C. Boer (Berlin, 1888), and the saga of Egill the One-Handed and Ásmundr the Slayer of Berserks: *Egils saga einhenda ok Ásmundar berserksbana*, in *Drei Lygisögur*, ed. Åke Lagerholm (Halle, 1927).

A helpful article by Peter Jorgensen is 'The Two-troll Variant of the Bear's Son Folk Tale in *Hálfdanar saga brönufóstra and Gríms saga loðinkinna*', in *Arv: Journal of Scandinavian Folklore*, XXXI (1975), pp. 35–43.

For *Jómsvíkinga saga*, I consulted the edition of Carl af Pettersens, *Jomsvíkinga saga efter Arnamagnæanske handskriften N:o. 291.4:to.* (Copenhagen, 1882).

For the First Grammatical Treatise, I consulted the edition of Hreinn Benediktsson, *The First Grammatical Treatise: Introduction, Text, Notes, Translation, Vocabulary, Facsimiles* (Reykjavík, 1972).

Sturla þáttr is found in *Íslendinga sögur og – þættir*, ed. Bragi Halldórsson et al. (Reykjavík, 1987).

The medieval Norwegian laws are collected in the monumental edition *Norges gamle love indtil 1387*, put together by a team of scholars in the nineteenth century. I have cited provisions from both the Gulaþing and Borgarþing codifications.

Historia Norwegiae is available in both the original Latin and English translation, with very helpful commentary material, in *Historia Norwegiae*, ed. Inger Ekrem and Lars Boje Mortensen, trans. Peter Fisher (Copenhagen, 2003).

On trolldom, witchcraft and magic, see Catharina Raudvere, '*Trolldómr* in Early Medieval Scandinavia', in *Witchcraft in Europe*, vol. III: *The Middle Ages* (London, 2002), pp. 73–169.

Finnboga saga ramma is edited by Jóhannes Halldórsson in vol. XIV of the series Íslenzk fornrit (Reykjavík, 1959).

The episode of Snorri being rescued by Bishop Guðmundr is in *Guðmundar sögur biskups*, ed. Stefán Karlsson (Copenhagen, 1983).

Because the sagas of Olaf Tryggvason take many forms, different titles are used to distinguish them. The 'great saga' is a late culmination of the tradition, called 'great' because of its length. It was edited by Ólafur Halldórsson in *Ólafs saga Tryggvasonar en mesta*, 3 vols (Copenhagen, 1958– 2000). The episode in question is in vol. II (1961).

Þiðreks saga was edited by Guðni Jónsson (Reykjavík, 1962).

Halldórs þáttr I was edited by Einar Ól. Sveinsson in Íslenzk fornrit 5 (Reykjavík, 1934).

Grænlands annáll was edited by Ólafur Halldórsson in *Grænland í miðaldaritum* (Reykjavík, 1978).

Flóamanna saga was edited by Þórhallur Vilmundarson and Bjarni Vilhjálmsson, in Íslenzk fornrit 13 (Reykjavík, 1991).

The Old Swedish story of the mother of St Bartholomew was edited by George Stephens in *Ett fornsvenskt legendarium*, vol. I (Stockholm, 1856). The Old Swedish *Konung Alexander* was edited by Gustaf Kleming: *Konung Alexander: en medeltidsdikt från latinet vänd i svenska rim* (Stockholm, 1862).

The text from *Encomion regni daniæ* is found in Kurt Weibull, 'Den lundensiska Finnsägnen' (*Fataburen*, 1908), pp. 29ff. (accessed at runeberg.org/fataburen/1908). The story of the gods, the master builder and Loki is found in the *Gylfaginning* section of Snorri Sturluson's *Edda*, trans. Faulkes, pp. 35–6.

The translation from Olaus Magnus is from *Olaus Magnus. Description of the Northern Peoples* [Rome, 1555], trans. Peter Fisher and Humphrey Higgens, ed. Peter Foote, 3 vols (London, 1998), vol. II, p. 299.

3 Folklore Trolls

The older collections of legends and tales cited include: Andreas Faye, *Norske sagn* (Arendal, 1833); Jón Árnason, *Íslenskar þjóðsögur og æventýri*, 2 vols (Leipzig, 1862–4), new edn ed. Árni Böðvarsson and Bjarni Vilhjálmsson, 6 vols (Reykjavík, 1954–61); Bengt af Klintberg, *Svenska folksägner* (Stockholm, 1972); P. A. Säve, *Gotländska sägner*, ed. Herbert Gustavson (Uppsala, 1959–61); Evald Tang Kristensen, *Danske sagn. Some de har lydt i folkeminde* (Copenhagen, 1928–39); Waldemar Liungman, *Sveriges sägner i ord och bild*, 7 vols (Stockholm, 1957–69) – vol. IV, from which I quote a story, contains 'legends about the small people underground'. I also quoted one story from Reidar Thoralf Christiansen, *Folktales of Norway* (Chicago, 1964).

Also, Gunnar Olof Hyltén-Cavallius, *Wärend och wirdarne: ett förök i svensk etnologi*, 2 vols (Stockholm, 1864–8).

Bengt Holbek and Iørn Piø, *Fabeldyr og sagnfolk* (Copenhagen, 1967), is an entertaining presentation of all sorts of supernatural beings intended for a Danish popular audience.

The catalogues to which I refer are the following: Bengt af Klintberg, *The Types of the Swedish Folk Legend* (Helsinki, 2010); Lauri Simonsuuri, *Typen- und Motiv- Verzeichnis der finnischen mythischen Sagen* (Helsinki, 1961); Simonsuuri and Marjatta Jauhiainen, *The Type and Motif Index of Finnish Legends and Memorates* (Helsinki, 1998); Reidar Thoralf Christiansen, *The Migratory Legends. A Proposed List of Types with a Systematic List of the Norwegian Variants* (Helsinki, 1961).

The study of kidnapping by H. F. Feilberg to which I refer is *Bjergtagen* (Copenhagen, 1919).

The old Swedish proverbs are originally from Chr. Grubb, *Svenska ordsedher* (1604). I took them from Pelle Holm, *Ordspråk och talesätt* (Stockholm, 1965).

On Eve and Lilith see Virginia Geddes, *Various Children of Eve (AT 758): Cultural Variants and Antifeminine Images* (Uppsala, 1986).

4 Fairy-tale Trolls and Trolls Illustrated

The stories of Asbjørnsen and Moe are available in a great many editions. Rather than cite the specific editions I consulted, in this chapter I usually just give the title of the tale, in Norwegian and in English translation.

The formal classification of fairy tales, including the category 'Tales of the Stupid Ogre', goes back ultimately to the catalogue by the Finnish scholar Antti Aarne, *Verzeichnis der Märchentypen* (Helsinki, 1910). This was a catalogue of 'types' – that is, recurrent plots – that Aarne was able to isolate from a study of materials in Nordic folklore archives. He called such tales 'Märchen vom dummen Teufel (Riesen)' ('Tales of the Stupid Devil [Giant]'). When Aarne's catalogue was expanded and translated into English by the American folklorist Stith Thompson, first in 1928 and later expanded by Thompson and subsequently by others, giant and devil were collapsed into the stupid ogre.

The quotation from Erik Werenskiold is found in his *Samtlige tegninger og studier til Norske folkeeventyr ved P. Chr. Asbjørnsen, Jørgen Moe og Moltke Moe* (Kristiana and Copenhagen, 1910) (pages not numbered), which can be recommended in general for a collection of his illustrations to Asjørnsen's and Moe's tales.

Several books collect Theodor Kittelsen's illustrations. Among them I can mention Leif Østby, *Theodor Kittelsen: Tegninger og akvareller/Drawings and Watercolours* (Oslo 1993), which includes the suggestion of a self-portrait in the troll on Karl Johan Street, and *Theodor Kittelsen i tekst, tegninger og malerier* (Oslo, 1945), which gathers not only illustrations but also text by Kittelsen.

The new (second) edition of Asbjørnsen's (and Moe's) *Udvalgte eventyr*, with Kittelsen's frontispiece, was published in Kristiana (Oslo) in 1907.

A lively treatment of the progression from Eckersberg to Werenskiold and Kittelsen is offered by JoAnn Conrad, '"This Is What Trolls Really Look Like": The Folklore That Is Norway', in *News from Other Worlds: Studies in Nordic Folklore, Mythology and Culture*, ed. Timothy R. Tahgnerlini and Merrill Kaplan (Berkeley, CA, 2012).

Bland tomtar och troll has been published continuously since 1907. Many famous authors and illustrators have been found in its pages over the years. A piece of trivia is that one of the later illustrators was Gustaf Tenggren (1896–1970), who emigrated to the United States and had a career as an illustrator of children's works. He was employed for a time by the Walt Disney company and contributed in 1937 to *Snow White and the Seven Dwarfs*, the first animated full-length film.

Two works that give a good idea of John Bauer's style are *John Bauer: Bland tomtar och troll. Trettio bilder i mezzotypi till Ett urval bland tomtar och troll åren 1907–1915* (Stockholm, 1918), and *John Bauers bästa: ett urval sagor ur bland tomtar och troll åren 1907–1915* (Stockholm [no date]).

Born in Geneva, Paul Henri Mallet (1730–1807) was based in Copenhagen in the middle of the eighteenth century. Especially the second part of his *Introduction à L'histoire du Danemarch où l'on traite de la religion, des moeurs, des lois, et des usages des anciens Danois* (1755), namely *Monuments de la mythologie et de la poesie des Celtes, et particulierement des anciens Scandinaves* (1756), was internationally well known and translated into English by Bishop Percy in 1770. There are giants aplenty, but no trolls.

Hans Christian Andersen's tales, which he published over many years, are only a part of his impressive and important literary output. The translation by Mrs Paull is silent on her given name(s): *Hans Andersen's Fairy Tales: A New Translation, by Mrs Paull. With a Special Adaptation and Arrangment for Young People* (London, 1867). The *Riverside Magazine for Young People* was an illustrated monthly published for a few years in New York.

5 Trolls in Literature

The 1940 quotation from Sigurd Hoel was gathered into his *Våre eventyr* (1948) and is quoted in Marte Hvam Hult, *Framing a National Narrative: The Legend Collection of Peter Christen Asbjørnsen* (Detroit, 2003), p. 23. Hult takes up some of the material I do here and, beyond that, she is well worth reading for her analysis of how Asbjørnsen's legend publications articulate with Norway's national narrative. On the Green-clad One, see p. 208, n. 20, where she quotes the Ibsen translator William Archer. As for Ibsen, I have made my own translations from a standard edition of the play, striving solely for accuracy rather than for actability. My reference to literary histories is specifically to that of Francis Bull, *Norsk litteraturhistorie*, vol. 1, p. 364. The quotation from Edmund Gosse is taken from *The Spectator*, 20 July 1872 (accessed at http://ibsen.nb.no/id/11167590.o).

The works of Ibsen and the other authors (Lie, Drachmann, Fröding, Aakjær, Lagerlöf, Ekman, Sinisalo) that I discuss in this chapter are widely available, and I have translated from readily available editions. Charles Wharton Stork's translation of 'Ett gammalt bergtroll' is from his *Anthology of Swedish Lyrics: From 1750 to 1915. Translated in the Original Meters* (New York and London, 1917).

I read about Boye's *Gorm den gamle* in an article by Anne-Marie Mai, 'Bland Nordens gudar, danska borgare och kungliga hjältinnor', *Kvinnornas litteraturhistorie* (http://nordicwomensliterature.net).

6 Trolls, Children, Marketing and Whimsy

There is of course a vast literature on fairy tales. The works I quote at the beginning of the chapter are these: Jack Zipes, 'Cross-cultural Connections and the Contamination of the Classical Fairy Tale', and Benedetto Croce, 'The Fantastic Accomplishment of Giambattista Basile and his Tale of Tales: *Lo cunto de li cunti* as a Literary Work' [1932], both in Jack Zipes, ed., *The Great Fairy Tale Tradition: From Straparola and Basile to the Brothers Grimm* (New York and London, 2001); Ruth Bottigheimer, *Grimms' Bad Girls and Bold Boys: The Moral and Social Vision of the Tales* (New Haven and London, 1987); Bengt Holbek, *Interpretation of Fairy Tales: Danish Folklore in a European Perspective* (Helsinki, 1987).

The long passage explaining how Yrjö Kokko met his Pessi and Illusia was translated by Kaarina Brooks and accessed at www.kaarinabrooks.com.

On Tove Jansson, see W. Gwyn Jones, *Tove Jansson* (Boston, MA, 1987) and Tove Holländer, *Från idyll till avidyll. Tove Janssons illustrationer till muminböckerna/From Idyll to Non-Idyll: An Analysis of the Illustrations in Tove Jansson's Moomin Books* ([Tammerfors], 1983).

D'Aulaires Trolls was first published in Garden City, NY, 1972 and was reprinted in 2006 by the *New York Review of Books* under the title *D'Aulaires Book of Trolls*.

All the quotations about the troll in the Oakland–San Francisco Bay Bridge are from www.baycitizen.org.

All the information quoted about the Fremont troll is from www.fremont.com.

Epilogue

Trolls in slang, and especially on the Internet, are definitely a moving target. While working on this book I found that within even a few weeks Internet links went dead, or similar searches led to different results. I have given the links that I used, but I cannot promise that they will lead the reader where they led me, or indeed that they will lead anywhere. Still, I think that the troll as a loser in slang, and the Internet troll as an anti-social abuser of the net, are usages that will continue to hold for some time to come.

Acknowledgements and Photo Acknowledgements

Although I had long contemplated writing a book of this nature, it was Ben Hayes who got me going on it; my thanks to him and the rest of the team at Reaktion. While conceiving and writing the book, I enjoyed the spirited discussions of the Wildcat Canyon Seminars in Berkeley. The draft was completed in the end of 2012, and I undertook the various revisions, completions, and checking in 2013, while I was a fellow at the Swedish Collegium for Advanced Study in Uppsala, working happily on another project. The Collegium provides a delightful and supportive environment for scholars, and the resources of the University of Uppsala library were essential and the staff unfailingly helpful. It is a pleasure to be able to signal my warm gratitude to both institutions so soon after completing my fellowship in Uppsala.

The photograph of 'Giant Finn' on p. 47 is by Anders Andrén, who, along with my other collaborator in Uppsala, Jens Peter Schjødt, helped make it such a rewarding and enjoyable year.

Index

page numbers in *italics* refer to illustrations